EVELYN,
  YOUR WORK
AND DEFINE
KEEP ON DOIN' WHAT YOU'RE
DOIN.

ALL THE BEST,

Steve Perry

The Window Pain

Renegade
Book

Cover design by Steve Perry

Printed and published by:
Renegade Books
40 Middlefield Street
Middletown, Connecticut 06457

Printed in the United States of America

ISBN: 0-9708929-0-X
Library of Congress Control Number: 2001116504

FOREWARD

I needed to write <u>The Window Pain.</u> When I started writing I didn't know why. Over time I realized that the reason I needed to write was because the stories that were pounding in my chest were not mine. Their relentlessness was inspired by their quest to get out and be given to you. Now they are free and in your hands. Use them as you will. It is my hope that you will learn from them, for they have taught me much about me and you.

As you read this you may find yourself wondering, 'Is this real? Did this really happen?' The answer to both questions is yes. I have seen what you will soon see with mine and/or borrowed eyes.

<u>The Window Pain</u> is not an autobiography, but I have bumped into its characters many times. As a result, this is some of the realest shit I have ever penned. Its words will take you down a path that leads to my soul and as you look at me you will recognize glimpses of yourself starring back.

For years I was afraid of the story's proximity to my own life. I feared that you, my friend, relative, stranger, supporter, coach, teacher, admirer, detractor would get to know me. You, that person who is not me, would get to know me in ways that I'm not sure that I have really gotten to know me. Then you could judge me and, because you were paying attention, you might be right and I'd have to accept your judgment.

I believe that the greatest art comes out of struggle. It begins as a notion, a drop of paint pressed against the page. Then it grows, bleeding like a watercolor, racing to the end of the paper. As its path is impeded by the wall of concepts previously pressed upon it, the new notion struggles. During this process, beauty is defined. As the idea twists and turns, it becomes art; exposing another piece of our soul. I have come to accept that, through this work, you will discover my route, get to know my struggle and the colors of my art.

When I first wrote <u>The Window Pain</u> I was afraid of you, afraid of how you'd look at me, my characters, my creation. I was scared of being held responsible for revealing family secrets or telling lies. So much has been entrusted in me. So many dreams have been pinned on my chest like a note that goes home from the kindergarten teacher. What if you felt that the note hadn't made it home and that the dream was carelessly left on a playground during a fierce game of kickball? Would that mean that I was a fraud, a failure whose potential was written on a note that was too big for me to carry? If I admitted to the validity of it all, would I ever be the man that you hoped I'd be? Could a man as imperfect as I lead, inspire or befriend you?

Now I am no longer stymied by what I think you 'might' think. Writing allowed me to create my own world where I played by rules that didn't need to make sense to anyone but me. I like it there. I bet you'd like it there too. This is why I'm inviting you in by giving you back your stories.

I have woven the lives of my students, friends, family and strangers to patch together this story. Through them I have explored some of the social and personal issues that haunt me. As a social worker I am free to listen and write reports "objectively". I am also free to run from my own demons while *ghost busting* on behalf of others. <u>The Window Pain</u> has freed me of my ghost busting responsibilities for the moment. Now I can begin to address the Stay Puff Marshmallow Man that troubles me. This freedom to explore my full humanity is invigorating and cathartic.

Do I hope that you like what I've written? Hell yeah, especially if you paid for it. What is more important to me though is that as you read <u>The Window Pain,</u> the stories and characters, help you to feel, hear, see and taste some of life's complexities.

ACKNOWLEDGEMENTS

I used to tell people that I wrote this book so that I could do the 'Acknowledgements'. I felt I had a lot to say and prove to a lot of people. Over the five years that have passed since the completion of this work, I amassed a list of 'thank yous' and an equal sized list of 'f-yous'. It was in this section that I had planned to launch into my barrage of love and lash. I was going to focus it on those most notable and notorious in my life. Then I was given today.

Today is Columbus Day, 2000. I had the day off. For the most part, it was filled with chores. It's not hard to fill a day this way when you live in a house that was built in 1924. I cut the lawn, well most of it, did the laundry, well, most of it and I painted an exterior door red, I finished that.

As I moved from bed to bath, garage to basement, living room to porch in the delightful chill of a New England fall, a rhythm and focus overcame me. When I finally looked at my watch after hours of painstakingly working to avoid dripping red paint on the porch I noticed that it was 5:00 p.m. I realized that I had made it through yet another day.

Now that the door is painted, grass is nearly mowed and we have clean clothes for tomorrow, I am reminded that the most important thing that I can do with the 'Acknowledgements' is to give thanks. I will leave the f-yous for another day and another author. This author, today, is hell-bent on thanking God for His glory, mercy and the angels He has used to touch my life. I am daunted by the notion that there will be a time when there are more pasts than presents, more yesterdays than tomorrows. When that time comes, I hope to have spent most of my days glorifying Him and making His angels proud of me. His mercy humbles me.

If I forget anyone, please know that it is my mind, not my heart that is to blame.

I will begin by acknowledging those people who, for reasons

only God knows, have touched me in ways I cannot and will not explain. To them, I give my sincerest thanks.

Mom, thank you. For the most part, it's been just the two of us. You have been my friend, my enemy, my hope, and my inspiration. Santa gave the Salvation Army one toy and one dress to pass on to you. Your teens brought you an abusive boyfriend and husband. Ignorance got you pregnant. Racism made them abandon us. Courage helped you raise a son and you gave me a reason to live. Thank you ma'. I know I don't say it enough, but your boy has got a problem with his heart. In that place where there is the greatest depth of love, the door sometimes sticks. Please know that everyday that I live, I do love you, I do appreciate you and I promise you that one day I will make you proud.

Grandma Perry, Grandma Lucy, Grandpa and Grand Daddy, thank you. Your lives, and Grandma Perry, your death, have brought me some of my greatest joys and sorrows. I have seen you love until it hurt. I have watched as you gave each of your children everything that you ever had and then borrowed when that wasn't enough. I also watched as you slept at the dinner table out of complete exhaustion. I have seen you cry. I have patiently corrected you as you rattled off the names of my cousins, brothers and uncles before you got to 'Stevie'. You have welcomed everyone who came into your home and as you filled them with food, you stuffed them with stories of every good thing that anyone of us ever did, even if you had to embellish. Your caring hands have washed me in the sink and embraced me as if you hadn't seen me in years. Thank you all. Grandma Perry and Grandpa, I miss you. Grandma Lucy and Grand daddy, I revel in you.

Annette, Jake, Eva Mae, Harvey, Janice, Stella, Liz, Mike, Gary, Nym and Van, thanks for helping my mother raise me. Tuddie, Pam, Stephanie, Wayne, Bell, G, Terry, Barbara, Pooh, Keith, Jeffrey, Junior, DD, Tammy, Felicia and Jackie, thanks for making being raised so much fun. Sean, B.J., Danielle, Jamie, Little Jeffrey, Brandon, Derrick, Corey, Dominique, Desmond, Devon and all of my little cousins, prepare yourselves to be thoughtful men and women and you will have lots of fun.

Mr. and Mrs. Saunders, Mr. Kennsel, Peter Budryk, Dr. John McCray, Jr. and Dr. Peter Vaughn, thank you for educating me. Fult-Dog, (Chris Fulton), J.G., (Julani Ghana), Cle, (Cleon Francis), thanks for educating me on how to have fun. Baye Wilson, thank you for being there when nobody from where I was at knew where I was coming from and nobody from where I was from was where I was at.

Thank you, Yusuf Salaam. You have been a spiritual guide, pain in my ass and one of the people I most admire. The way you effortlessly love your wife and daughter makes me want to be a better man.

Thank you Nicole Curtis. Ever since we went our separate ways I'd wondered how I would acknowledge you. Ninety-nine percent of this book was written in our relationship, in our apartment. Since then, much has been affected by our parting; my clothes, my toothbrush, etc.. Much has also happened for us, degrees, marriage, etc. In all Stink, I wish you happiness. Thank you for your support. I do not think I could have done this without you.

Thank you Kenny, or as grandma would say it, 'Cuddin Kenny P. Ours is an unspoken language. We have been through more than either of us, or our wives, would like to acknowledge. From the projects, through going to a motel to escape domestic violence, back to previewing motels as a last stop on a date, up to tonight, when we are days away from the birth of your first son, we have grown upward and inward. Damn, it's been a trip. You have been my moral compass and my guide through a few treks into immorality. Thank you for being the greatest friend that my life has ever seen.

Thank you Lalani. No one knows more than you that I am as cuddly as a porcupine and wrought with inconsistencies, yet you decided to be my wife. You have embarked upon a voyage towards eternal happiness with me, the prince of pessimism. Although over 50% of those who begin this journey fail, you greet me every morning with a childlike optimism. You are my sunshine. In us, I have found focus lost, only to again find my focus.

There have been times that we've bucked so much that I never thought we'd get out of first gear. Through it all though, you have had the courage to believe in the unbelievable, see the invisible and the strength to have faith in us. I see so much of my mother in you. That both scares and excites me. It scares me because I know she can get on my nerves. It excites me because she gives me life. Lalani, you are showing me how to love. Outside of life itself, this is the greatest gift of all. Thank you.

Last but not least, daddy, thank you. I hope that your life is all that you'd hoped it would be. I have learned much from you. I wish you all the best.

Table of Contents

The Window Pain
Chapter 1

Like the crash of mighty cymbals, the flying vase exploded the unsuspecting window into thousands of solidified raindrops. The force of the collision propelled shards of glass onto the coarse surface of the sidewalk below where they tingled like wind chimes caressed by a gentle mid afternoon summer breeze. Scattered across the sidewalk together in a tragic memorial, the vase and the window were mere fragments of their former selves. The two independent objects had both become victims of the moment's rage.

This was the crescendo of chaos in a dance of terror. Fists had flailed while bodies crashed into one another and anything else that was near by. This trail of chaos started in a place called insecurity, spun into suspicion and crashed into anger. The sounds that it made broke into my dreams and snatched me into a morning fog. As I rubbed my eyes, a sense of familiarity crept in. It was in many ways a day like many other days. I was ten and this was yet another time when I found myself lying in bed, watching a tornado of familiar faces spin out of control outside of my sharpening vision.

The combatants were my parents, Jennifer and Tarique Oakman, Sr. I'd spent those first ten years loving them unconditionally. Sure, I hated what they did to each other. I especially hated what my father did to my mother, but, up until that fight, she was my mother and he was my father and that was all that mattered.

As the last remnants of the window dangled and then, piece by piece, dripped onto the sidewalk, they both stood there silent, out of breath and hurt pretty bad. Only the awakening of the city and an occasional breeze finding its way through the newly opened front picture window would interrupt this Saturday.

Each of their Saturday morning brawls began like any familiar symphony. My mother's high-pitched voice entered like the string section, swaying back and forth, setting the tone of the piece. Then my father's persistent percussion would answer her gentle strings. There the two began, back and forth, up and down. At first they'd rely on the message in their notes to carry the piece. Then, seemingly all at once, crash! The melody would change. It became an orchestral confrontation. She'd scream, as the bows were pressed harder and harder against her already burning strings. Not to be outdone, his powerful percussion predictably answered with his first instinct, to bang, crash, kick and bellow. My father thought that in order to be heard, it wasn't the value of the note, it was how hard he hit the skins. Slamming, banging, screaming until, filled with emotion and a deep loathing for their musical foe, they both would put all they had into one final stanza, and then, BANG! It was over. There they stood, both exhausted and vanquished.

Sometimes I'd wonder if a week could pass without them fighting. These two people who were adult enough and "in love" enough to bring a son into this world seemed to be on some type of woop ass clock. It was as if some damn horn went off in their heads and, just like the Road Runner and Wil-e-Coyote, they'd start droppin' anvils on each other. Unlike that silly Coyote though, there were times when my father would actually catch my mother.

As the smoke cleared on that particular brawl, I wondered if my parents had ever really loved each other like normal people. It amazed me how the relationships I was growing up around almost always ended up like this. I mean, it's not like everybody beat each other up, but you don't have to hit somebody to hurt them. Saying things like, "I can't stand you," to the mother of your child can sever the heart of even the most committed woman. Cheating, staying out all night, and other forms of disregard steadily floated into the relationships around me and flourished in their fertile soils of discontent.

I remember wondering if my mother ever put my father's cologne on her stuffed animals to smell him when he wasn't around. Did he have a song that reminded him of her? I thought about what it would have been like if my parents had pet names for each other? I didn't care if they were creative ones. Honey, babe, or darling would do. I even tried to imagine a time when they solved an argument by saying 'okay, I'm sorry' instead of beating each other into submission. I just wanted to know if there ever was a time when they acted civilized towards each other. If there was, what happened?

I couldn't accept that my mother, an intelligent, beautiful, black woman, just one day decided to be in a bad relationship. The transition into the life that she was living had to be gradual. It defies logic that she was walking down the street and my father came up, hit her on the head, dragged her back to his cave and has since held her captive. No, she wanted to be with him. I'd heard her say it. She'd say she loved him. She'd talk about the good old days. But damn, was it just a few days that were good? And, were they so good that they compensated for this shit?

Maybe there was a time when she did put his cologne on a stuffed animal and he mistook the scent for that of another man and, in his rage, he grabbed her. Then, shocked that her Romeo had gotten physical with her, she cried. He probably joined her and the two held long into the night, made love, and together they mended the shaken foundation of her trust. On an emotional high, it was probably shortly after this that he asked her to marry him. She loved him. She loved the idea of being with him. She loved the idea of being married. He was a take-charge kind of man. No shit from nobody was how she saw him. He had to be sincere, she must have thought. She knew that he would never treat her like that again. He did. Maybe it was immediately after that first incident or perhaps it took a few months, I'm not sure, but this time I bet he actually hit her. It would have probably been after an argument, one in which he blamed her for taking it too far. She loved him. She trusted him. She must have believed him. It must have felt like it was her fault. She knew that she could be argumentative, besides, he had to love her. She loved him. She loved being married. She loved being married to him. He was a good man. He went to work each day and she wanted for nothing. Well, nothing but affection, kind words, to feel special, to not be humiliated in public or berated at home, but men didn't show too much affection, at least that's what he said, and that other stuff, she knew that he wasn't like that all of the time.

On that day, you know, the one when she really believed him, the erosion of her self-esteem had begun. It was slow, steady and effective. It took a while for her foundation of self-respect to completely erode. The absolute demise of my mother's self-respect began when she tried to understand and then accept that my father could hit and love her in the same day.

It didn't take long for my mother's self-esteem to become a distant memory. She was now numb to his assaults on her. Not only was she numb, but, in an effort to make sense of it all, or maybe it was out of a deep shame, she found herself defending her husband, her marriage and her bruises. When others noticed the scratches and scars around her neck, she'd muster a smile and assured them that she was okay and, "If I wasn't, I'd tell you or I'd leave." I'm sure they wanted to believe her as much as she wanted to believe herself. They didn't though and I don't think she did either.

All I ever wanted was for things to be simple in my life, like on TV. I wanted to live in a world where parents acted like the Bradys and kids like me only had to worry about being kids. I did my part to make this world real. I had a mangy, barely stuffed bear with one eye named Teddy that I took everywhere. I named him after Teddy Pendergrass. My mother loved him, well actually, everybody's mother loved him. I suppose I could have named him Marvin, all the mommies loved him too, but he wasn't as cool. Anyway, I only cared about mine and she loved Teddy like that, then, I could love my bear the same way. The only problems me and Teddy had was when I couldn't remember where I'd left him. I never dreamed of beating him up. He meant too much to me.

As a ten year old black boy growing up in the 70's, I derived my moral conviction from a black and white floor model television set.

It seems like it went into a vertical hold frenzy during the best part of every show. The TV had no knobs, so the channel changer was a pair of lock pliers and I was the remote control. As I lay on my stomach on the floor, my father would tap my foot with his and I would dutifully make my way to the set to change the channel or mess with the aluminum foil antenna. The TV's convex screen was flanked by two gold, cloth covered speakers. I trusted the characters because they were there for me when all I had was Teddy. They were friends. Through the enormous window, I was taught to count by a white-haired mustached Captain named after a marsupial and I learned the dynamics of relationships from the Funtastic world of Hana-Barbera. Within the picture tube, Fred never threatened to blow Wilma's fuckin' head off if she didn't finish the dishes before he got home from the gravel pit. I never saw Weezy double over because George had kicked her in the stomach. And I know I never saw the Brady kids act like they were sleeping to avoid hearing the crack of Mike's fist against Carol's jaw.

So when I saw so much violence between my parents, it created a perceptual dilemma in my young mind. I couldn't understand why every issue in my life was solved by yelling and fighting while the people on TV solved everything by talking. Not even the Fonz hit people. The only answer I could come up with to explain the inconsistency was that Fred and Wilma, George and Weezy, Bradys and even the Fonz were all fakes. But could my friends have lied? Could the characters on TV, my baby-sitters, teachers and playmates have led me astray?

On TV everything was resolved in thirty minutes, including commercials. Never was an issue left unfinished, unless you're including the soaps, but who watched that junk? It was simple on TV. The bad guys wore black and usually died in time for a moral to be spelled out for the audience. It didn't happen this way in my house. As I became more and more conscious of things around me, what happened in the lives beyond the convex looking glass began to appear fuzzy and distorted. It became hard to accept what the TV was showing me.

According to the world in which I lived, real people got mad.

And when they got too mad, there was no commercial break. No one talked it over or listened. People yelled. At times it seemed like everybody was yelling at somebody for something. Everybody yelled. "Get over here!," when I got caught in the candy aisle daydreaming about the 'peanut buttery nougat' hiding within the bed of chocolate. My parents yelled when they were happy, mad or even when they were confused, 'What did you say?' Their raised voices would dive into the ears of their target and go straight for its heart. The intonation that had catapulted their voices ensured that their words would leave a wound.

Anita and Les Sanders lived up the street from us. They were two people who treated each other like the people on TV. They were kind of like Florida and James Evans, Jr. from "Good Times". Mr. Sanders was a tall brown skinned man with a husky build who used to be pretty good in basketball, but since high school he had a few operations on his knees. Now he works at the University of Pennsylvania as a janitor. Mrs. Sanders was about 5' 4" and she wore her hair long. She was a secretary in a doctor's office in Center City. They have two sons and a daughter. Everybody said their youngest son was going to be a doctor because he was so smart.

O.D., a small time drug dealer on my block, would tell me that the reason Mr. and Mrs. Sanders treated each other the way they did was because they weren't really black. O.D. was short for Odicious, which only his mother could safely call him. He sold nickel bags of weed and on occasion he'd get his hands on some cocaine or heroin. His slim build, grayish complexion and big afro made him look like a microphone. He drove a baby blue Ninety Eight and carried a .22 in his brown zip-up patent leather platform boots. He would have done anything to protect the corner of 36th and Mt. Vernon. It was his whole world. Being small time made O.D. dangerous.

O.D. used to call Mr. Sanders a punk. I could hear the disgust in his voice when he'd say, "Sanders lets her do whatever she wants. He ain't got no control over his ol' lady!" Back then even a young girlfriend was an 'ol lady'. The main reason O.D. called Mr.

Sanders a punk was because his wife was going to the Community College of Philadelphia. To support her, Mr. Sanders stayed home with their kids. "The woman is supposed to be at home takin' care of the kids." O.D. said, "A real black man wouldn't be changin' no damn diapers or workin' overtime while his wife goes to school at night to learn about computers." One of his favorite phrases was, "White people go to college, black people clean 'em." In his eyes, being a janitor at Penn was the only indication that Mr. Sanders was black or a man.

One day O.D. and I were talking and he asked me, "If Mrs. Sanders is goin' to college and Mr. Sanders is at home takin' care of the kids, what color is 'dey and what sex is he?" I just looked at him because I didn't have a clue as to what in the hell he was talking about. He could tell I was confused so he said, "Don't worry little man, you'll figure it out." O.D. felt that Black people were tarred by the Creator and feathered with the ghetto. He'd tell me that Black people were being punished for some unforgivable sin that none of us were old enough to remember committing. According to him, Judgment had been passed. He said our existence was our sentence and our neighborhood was our prison. He told me that, "Not only do we live in Hell, but when we die we're goin' to another one." This is why he said he sold drugs. He said he was going to have as much fun as possible in this hell before he died and had to go to the one waiting for him. O.D. tried to make it clear that as Black people we are scarred by our hue, "Black people can't escape from Hell." Escaping was exactly what O.D. saw the Sanders trying to do. He used to say, "You can't run from yourself, 'cause no matter where ya' go there ya' are. The Sanders are trying to run into a world that don't exist." To him there was no 'Promise Land' for black people. "The only things that are real are the ones you can touch."

What O.D. said made sense to me. On TV and in my neighborhood, Blacks were catching hell. When I thought about it, everybody came home from work dirty and tired. Backs ached, hands were rock hard and work clothes would have to be left outside just so the stench of the underclass could evaporate enough to be put in the washing machine. Almost everybody who could find work did work. Women, men, kids, everybody was doing something to pay the bills, even O.D. would get real jobs from time to time. There was no herd of happy welfare heifers. We were doing what we had to do to 'keep our heads above water and make a wave where we could' but it didn't seem to matter because right around every corner were, "Temporary layoffs…" Even on TV our greatest black men and women portrayed slaves, like on "Roots" or pimps, prostitutes and drug dealers, like on "Starsky and Hutch". If it wasn't for Kunta Kinte and Huggie Bear there wouldn't have been any black 70's TV stars. None of these black people looked anything like the Sanders.

O.D. seemed to give up on the whole 'job thing' after a while. Even when he was working, his life was built around his next hustle. He was driven by his pursuit of personal pleasure and I idolized him for it. I wanted to be just like him. I loved his Ninety Eight. It had fuzzy dice hanging from the rearview mirror and in the back window there was a dog whose head bounced non-stop. His eight track player never skipped so he didn't need any match books sticking out of his dash board. Its baby blue flesh was only interrupted by pin stripes that went from bumper to bumper. It had a TV antenna perfectly fixed on the trunk. The air inside was polluted by trees and naked lady air freshners. O.D.'s sleek mother ship, fueled by blood that trickled from our community's syringe scarred arms, floated through the neighborhood. In my eyes, he was the richest man alive. He was the emperor of our block, King Midas with an afro. He had it all on a block that had nothing to give, he lived the lifestyle of the rich and worthless.

O.D. was the coolest man I knew. I'd sit at his feet and marvel at his stories. I hung on his words, climbed the obstacles he painted and nestled my head comfortably in the bosoms of his every conquest. He was my ghetto superhero. When I talked to him I felt like I was listening to fables spun by my very own Brown Hornet and Super Fly incarnate. He had all the ladies and nobody messed with him. He was the man. He was a bad motha', you know the rest. He'd pull up behind me on my way home from school, honk his horn, which went on for about 10 seconds, and say, "Git in young blood." We'd ride around for hours. Even when we just sat there, I felt like a prince. The kids in school knew that I hung with O.D. and they idolized me for it. He told me that I could take over the block in a few years, but I had to learn how to run things. He promised to teach me everything he knew about selling and handling the ladies. "You ain't supposed to treat a woman too good, because then she'll think she can do whatever she wants." "So," he told me, "you got to take care of bidness 'by any means necessary', jus' like Malcolm said." He made a lot of sense. This wasn't the first time I'd heard this. These words echoed through the blown-out buildings on my block and then rattled the windows in my living room. Although what O.D. said wasn't how relationships looked on TV, it was the mirror image of the 3600 block of Mt. Vernon, my world.

I never had to look far to see women being mistreated, mainly because my father didn't know how to treat his wife. He didn't romance her or even as much as talk to her. When he'd get home my mother couldn't get him to mumble one kind word. No 'hey babe, how was your day?' Not even a 'Food smells good, what 'er we havin'?' Nothing. On a good day, she'd get a 'Hey.' Those 'Hey' days were the good ones. That was when I felt like we were a family. By the time dinner hit the table, we'd be talking about how we were gonna move out of Philly to somewhere like Delaware. My father would talk for hours about 'getting' up out of Philly. "This ain't no place to raise my son. We could git us a nice house in Dover and not have to worry 'bout these crazy niggas 'round here." Both my mother and I excitedly followed him on his fantasies to Delaware.

"Daddy, will I have my own room?"

"Hell yeah. A big one. You my boy, I'm gonna give you the world. You gonna have a yard, some trees, man it's gonna be beautiful. Ain't it?" The last part of that was directed at my mother. He never called her by her name. I don't know why. He just didn't. But, she usually knew when he was talkin' to her.

"I can't wait," she'd say. I don't know if she really couldn't wait or if she was just happy not to be fighting. Those 'Hey' days seemed to invigorate us all, validate the notion of family, give us a reason to smile. But then there were those other days. The days when simply being in the same house as him gave him the right to do whatever he felt was necessary to get what he wanted. On those days, nothing was out of bounds for him. He'd curse my mother, manipulate her and if neither of these got him what he wanted, he'd kick her ass.

Do you know what it's like to wake up to the sound of your mother gurgling for air because your father has his knee across her throat? Do you know how it feels to watch this happen to the very woman who gave birth to you, tucks you in at night and plays "This little piggy" with your toes? The same person who patiently washed off your tongue when, for some reason, you decided to eat the soap while you took a bath. Have you ever seen your mother crawling away, using her last bit of strength, not to beg her assailant, your father, to spare her the life which hangs by a feeble thread, but to remind her husband, your father, the one looming over her twisted frame, that if he doesn't stop the baby will hear? There may not be a more helpless feeling for a child whose only comfort is a raggedy brown bear.

Standing at the top of the stairs, peering around my slightly opened bedroom door, I could see this proud woman cower in the corner in a fetal position as my father kicked her and commanded her to, "Get the hell up! Stand on your feet! Stop crying, and take it like a woman!" Most kids have to go to the movies to see a pimp beat his bitch like this. All I needed to do was wake up to witness this nightmare.

It's a strange thing to wake up to a nightmare. To pray before you go to bed for a new five speed bike with banana seat, sissy bar and a Saturday morning in which the only yelling you'll hear will be "Yabba Dabba Dooo!" The bike never made it and the TV was never loud enough for me to hear Fred Flintstone over my parents.

The menacing hand of domestic violence had cast its shadow over our lives. Too often it would splash down on my mother's face. When it did, like a powerful midnight ocean wave, her skin became rippled and swollen black and a deep blue, with peaks of thick opaque yellowish white foam. Then her eyes would explode with a mist of tears as if the wave had collided with an awaiting unforgiving rock on shore.

That Saturday morning my eyes had once again seen the destruction of the petite woman who'd given birth to me at sixteen. To close them would do nothing more than transfer the savage beating to another of my senses. What my eyes could not see, my ears filled in the blanks. Even at ten years old, there was nothing new about watching this frantic scramble for position. I'd seen my mother's jaw that shade of purple before and the blood that ran down my father's cheek took a familiar path down his lips, over his chin, eventually dripping off his face, painting his shirt with little red tear drops. The only thing that was different about this particular Saturday morning brawl was that for the first time, I was able to pry the stifling hands of this grotesque spectacle from my heart just long enough to swear that, "I will never again let another man harm a woman I love!"

That morning, I couldn't stand at the top of the stairs. I could no longer peer. My stomach bubbled and my eyes overflowed with pure sorrow. I was paralyzed as I lay in my bed listening to my mother's unanswered screams for help. I thought to pray, but why? The bike, the Flintstones, were both lost in the night, wandering through the complexity of my family, afraid, like me, to enter my living room. "God, make it stop, please," I whispered with my hands clasped in front of my face. In the distance, I could still hear my mother's cries. "God, please make him stop," I had risen to my knees, hands still clasped, eyes begging the ceiling. In the distance, there were still cries. I fell to the bed, pulled my knees to my chest, put my hands over my ears and yelled, "God, pleeeease!!!" In the distance, cries. No one was listening, but that didn't matter to me anymore, because I was tired of that shit. I took my hands from my ears, defiantly wiped my eyes, stood up and swore that I would do whatever I had to do to make sure that nobody, not even my father would partake in this uncivilized maiming of another woman I loved. This ghastly display had swollen shut the eyes and mouths of everybody around me for too long; while it claimed the life and soul of the woman I loved. Not one person came to my mother's rescue that morning. Not even God.

It was amazing how numb our neighbors had become to acts such as these. My mother, father and I lived in the Mantua section of Philadelphia. Most people in Philly call it the 'Bottoms'. Everything and everybody is black in the Bottoms. Even the white lines in the streets were melting from the heat created by having so much black around them. Our block had row homes on both sides. Each was the same. The front door and a window were on the first floor. There were two windows on the second and two just like them on the third. The wooden boards put in each of the windows of each of the abandoned buildings were like hieroglyphics that told countless stories of abuse and violation. Chipped and cracked, they each were giving way to the stress of hopelessness that rose from beneath the smoldering asphalt.

Almost every other house was abandoned. This created a numbing symmetry. The black tar streets, with their gilded edged NO PARKING Zones, (which were never empty), had bottle caps and other metallic debris embedded in them. This caused the streets to look like studded black leather collars, pulled tight, asphyxiating an entire generation. We were caged in by dilapidated structures. Living under deplorable conditions with a few selfish and cruel people who robbed us all of our will to respond. Living with these individuals caused too many of us to lose the ability to react to even the most grotesque displays of human nature.

I wasn't the only child who wanted simplicity in his life. Different as we were from one to the other, we all did our best to have the opportunity to be consumed with childhood. The children in the Bottoms were like grass determined to grow through the cracks in the sidewalk. We'd play each day with the same intensity and love of life that they had in suburban Chestnut Hill. I guess if we'd listened for them, we could've even heard the birds chirping. We made do with the cards dealt to us and eventually created our own rules for the game. Living and playing with the stench left behind by a passing garbage truck, was incorporated into our childhood. The repugnant odor stopped us from fully inhaling, therefore the rules of the game became, "Okay, whoever stops holding their breath first is

IT, ready, set, go..." Every pothole and broken-down car was seen as a mere obstruction and without much thought they too became a part of the game, "You go down ten yards and at the pothole do a curl pattern, and you do a 'down and in' at Ms. Betty's broken-down car and I'll hit you by the big pothole."

We were kids plain and simple. The only job we wanted was to spend every second testing the limits of our existence. For us, all of life was a game and the only way to play it was to push it as hard as we could. Riding on handle bars and jumping off anything we could climb, with nothing more than a mattress and a pair of Pro Keds to protect us, was what life was all about. We didn't do things like this to bring death closer, we wanted to push life to its limits. As children we had no concept of death and therefore no fear of it. All we'd ever done was live and that was all we wanted to do. It was as if we had a subconscious goal to live our entire life before the streetlights came on.

We woke up earlier than the adults and tried to go to bed later. No day was taken for granted. Rain only meant we had to move the game inside. Snow meant we had to wear more clothes to play it. Sun meant we had to do it in the shade. And bedtime meant we had to play it so no one would hear us. Without the words of grown-ups like O.D., we would've never known that we were poor or black, because we were too caught up in trying to be kids.

During the day the Bottoms' streets were where kids pretended to be professional athletes and entertainers. At night, mostly on the weekends, the tar and asphalt became the stage where a few grown-ups acted out their roles as drug dealers and prostitutes. As the summer streets cooled from the combination of the sun's rays and the friction from children's feet, the actors entered one by one under flickering streetlights. The first to enter was always Latrice. She was as wide as she was tall and her high-pitched voice made everyone answer everything she said with, "Will you please shut up!" As she stood in the puddle of light raining from the streetlight above, her skin looked as smooth as oil, especially in the summer.

On Friday and Saturday nights I'd sneak out of bed and go over to my window after my mother tucked me in. I'd be there for hours kneeling with my forearms resting on my windowsill. The show that took place below my window was always better than TV. It had drama, suspense and more cuss' words than cable. I knew all the actors and the story line was unmatched. Prostitutes, pimps and preachers shared the same stage and urges. The show went on all night. All of the actors knew their roles and played them to perfection. The only one whose role I couldn't figure out was Latrice. She played many, but none of them required that she ever be too far away from a dick. I didn't know if she was a prostitute or if she was prostituting all of the other actors. All I knew was she had something they wanted and when they had something she wanted, she was open for business.

Latrice had a recurring role in this street opera, which meant she was on the street more than the white lines. O.D. was the other constant. The rest of the players came and went. As a matter of fact, most of them didn't even live in the Bottoms. They'd just get their stuff and go, like the drive-thru at McDonald's.

The most tragic result of the weekend show was when the exchange of intoxicating fluids between the actors lead to birth and a baby's fain't cry. Its mother was always a woman who'd gone a fifth too far on the Night Train as she tried to get to Ghetto Heaven. The baby's distant cry would rise from the horizon and hang in the sky, where it would signal the end of another performance and the beginning of another day. No matter what the actual calendar day was that the woman gave birth, we said that child was born on a Monday Mourning.

It was all part of the landscape. Latrice, O.D., the physical decay of our block, domestic violence and the silence that allowed them to flourish. These were all things the people who lived in the Bottoms came to expect. Everything had its place and everybody had a role from which they never veered. Although only ten, I knew it would take an act beyond any of our comprehension to knock our world off its axis. As a result of living under these conditions, our concept of what most consider reality was bizarre. Not even death could stop the methodical spinning of this world. For death itself was seen as an intricate part of life in the Bottoms. It was said that, "You can't die if you ain't lived."

As applause is to a symphony, so too were the tears that followed all of my parent's fights. The "I'm sorry's" and the "I love you, I swear I'll never do it again's," always seemed to wash the slate clean. This fight represented the end of my tolerance of blood shed. It also illuminated the impenetrable bond between my mother and me. And because blood stains, not even a Niagara Falls of my father's tears could wash away what he had done to our lives.

Normally, after-fight-clean-up usually followed the tears. This time, however, clean-up was going to take a little longer, because of the shattered window and vase on the sidewalk. Usually the clean-up took place after both of my parents went to their respective corners to take care of wounds they sustained during the bout. The time that the couple used taking care of their wounds was relative to how bad the fight was, but it usually preceded any apologies. Sometimes my father would apologize and swear he'd never do it again. Then they'd start cleaning up. Other times the order was reversed, clean up then apologize. The order was negotiable, but the elements were always the same.

This time, though, they broke the living room window and glass was everywhere. Therefore, with the physical clean-up being what it was, I was enlisted to man a broom outside on the stoop alongside my father. My mother would clean up inside. "Tarique!," my father called, "Git down here."

Acting like I slept through the storm, I said, "Okay dad," and came out of my room with Teddy in hand. Carefully I made my way down the stairs. I wasn't walking carefully because of the fight. It was because I had on my pajamas with the plastic feet in them. Everybody knows that one false move with those slippery plastic things on the bottom of my feet and I was through.

When I got downstairs I put on my blue Chuck Taylor's. Then my father and I went outside to clean up the front of our house. Before we got started he warned me to be careful, because, "Even after sweeping, there is always enough glass left over to cut you." He went on to say that, "You can never git all of the glass out of the sidewalk," so I swept very carefully.

Shortly after we got started, my father and I saw that Charles Hill, or "Hi C", as he liked to be called, and his girlfriend Lashana outside arguing again. Hi-C and 'Shanna, as everybody called her, had been together, if that's what you want to call what they were doing, for a while. For them, fighting was not confined to the weekends or their house. They would do it any day and anywhere. They'd come to your Spades game and if Shanna played that ace too early, ah man. They'd tear up the whole night. If money was involved, they might try to cut each other or anybody who'd try to break them up.

After arguing for a few minutes they started fighting. My father looked at them with disgust, "I don't understand 'dat nigga. He is always beatin' her ass out in tha street. Ain't Hi-C got no damn sense?" He went on to tell me that it's not so much that Hi-C was beating Shanna up, it's the how and where he was doing it. "Dere's a right way even to do somethin' wrong...One day you gonna learn," he told me, as I crouched down with an Ojay's album cover, (it doubled as a dust pan), tilted so that my father could start sweeping up the mess, "'dat life is all about decisions and one day you gotta decide whetha' you gonna be a man or jus' look like one. Tha's why I ain't sayin' nothin' 'bout Hi-C gettin' in Shanna's ass, 'cause you might have to do 'dat from time to time. Dass what being a man is all about, never lookin' like a sucka'." He continued to tell me that there is a proper way to, "take care of business." I took the first album cover full of broken glass and vase and put it in the garbage can.

"You gotta stand up for your pride and neva' let nobody make you look stupid or punk you off." I again knelt down so he could sweep up some more. "Women is jus' like men, they bof try you ta' see how long you gonna take it befo' you smack the shit outta' 'em. Tha's why if you smack 'em first, you ain't gotta worry 'bout 'em testing you, 'cause they already know you ain't got time for no games."

He paused for a second and put both hands on the top of the broom and interlocked his fingers. Then he rested his chin on top of his hands, "Hi-C is wrong cause he's smakin' Shanna out in the street. You supposed to keep yo business in tha' house, not out on tha' streets." I continued crouching on the sidewalk in anticipation of the next heap of vase and glass littering our front stoop. "Shanna gave up her life fo dat ugly nigga'," with that statement my father stopped sweeping all together. I was still crouching waiting for the next load.

"Shanna was ready to go to college befo' he knocked her up. Now 'dey got three bad ass, knotty head kids 'dat 'dey don't take care of," he started to sweep again. "And 'dat ain't it. That black bastard got another one runnin' roun' here too. He tries ta' say it ain't his, but everybody know it is."

Still talking and staring at Hi-C and Shanna, my father extended the broom for me to stand and take it. So I put down the O-Jays' album cover, stood up and took it. I guess the story was getting too good for him to be concerned with sweeping. He continued, "You know who his other baby is!" He pointed an accusing finger at me. I responded with a lifted brow of surprise. "Dat little fat black ass boy. He's bout yo' age, he looks jus' like Dracula. Now who else BUT Hi-C, tha' prince of darkness himself, looks like a burnt marshmallow wit' teef?" I kind of shrugged my shoulders, because I really didn't know the answer and I didn't think my father needed my answer to go on with the story. I was right, he didn't need my answer and the story rolled over my confusion. For some reason the day's lesson was 'the importance of every decision a person makes'. He leapt from one example to another of how making one bad decision can negatively impact your life for years. He stopped on a story about an encounter he had with a particular woman.

"Yeah, when ya' mother was pregnant wit' chu, 'dere was 'dis brown skinned chic 'dat I used to work wit' when I first started at UPS. She was my supervisor. All 'dat meant was 'dat she counted packages wit' a skirt on instead of a hot ass brown uniform." His demeanor was different than I'd ever seen it as he started this story.

"She wasn't really nothin' to look at. She thought 'dat her shit didn't stink and 'dat the whole world was jus' holdin' its breaf waitin' fo' her to show up." Apparently she'd gone to college for a few years and this was the best job she could get. He told me that this made her even madder at the world. In his words, "She had mo' attitude than a bee caught in a jar, 'dat was bein' shook up." He thought it was funny that she had gone to college and couldn't get a job much better than his. He said, "She was stuck in 'dat job like a wet tongue on a frozen pole." My father had a way with words that always made me laugh.

He always had something funny to say about everybody. He'd talk about the suit a man was wearing at his own funeral. He just didn't care. No one was safe from his comedic criticisms. He and I used to sit out on the stoop on summer days like that one for hours when he got home from work. Occasionally he'd send me in the house to get him another beer or up the street to Hickey's Hoagies on the corner of 36th and Haverford. We'd sit out there and laugh for hours. He could talk and so there was never a let up in his stand-up routine. He did impressions of people and his best was Richard Pryor's Mud Bone. I used to love when he did him. One day I asked him where babies came from and he said, "I don't know where 'DEY come from, but you came from two horny teenagers and a bottle of Mad Dog 20/20 while tha' Jackson Five was singing 'I'll be there' in the background." I always made sure that O.D. got me home in time to meet my dad. He really liked it that I was home to meet him. We had a routine we'd go through when he got home. First he'd say, "Where's my hug nigga?" Then I'd act like I forgot to hug him and then he'd say, "You ain't neva' gonna get too big for me to beat ya' ass." I'd smile and then hug him as if my life depended on it.

His story about the woman he worked with really started to get to him,. "Ta' me she was jus' somebody I knew. My life had no room fo' some flaky bitch who one day wanted ta' tell you her life story and tha' next ak like she couldn't remember ya' name. 'Dis bitch had Pre-PMS, PMS, Post-PMS and 'I'm mad cause I ain't got no PMS yet, PMS." Just then he stopped telling the story and looked around, almost as if he needed permission to continue. I don't know if he was looking for my mother or if he heard something. After a second or two he started patting himself down, feeling for his cigarettes.

"She KNEW I wasn't interested in screwing roun'. My lady was pregnant with my boy. I knew you was gonna be a boy and grow up to be jus' like me. Dat's why I named you Tarique Jr.,

after me. I had all I needed in my life. But she kept on houndin' me."
He finally found his cigarettes. He took one out, my father smoked
Benson and Hedges, put it between his lips, lit it, and took a long drag.
As his chest expanded I could almost see the satiny smoke fill his
lungs. Then he exhaled and went on. "She was a little older than me
and your mother," he started to count out loud, touching his fingers to
keep his place, "Let me see, Jennifer had you on, ...ummm and ahhhh,
so she was 'bout twenty one or so 'cause we was about sixteen when
you was born, right?" I knew it was a question, but I also knew it
wasn't for me to answer. He continued.

I could tell the story was reaching its moral conclusion because
his drags were getting stronger and more deliberate. He sat down on
the stoop and invited me to do the same by patting the cement beside
him. Even sitting down he never stopped talking. "She had 'dese big!,"
he put his hands up in front of his chest to show her cup size and then
he realized that I was too young to be talking about breasts. So he
smoothly brought his hands to his head and ran them on top of his thick
course hair and simply said, "Woo wee!" This said more than any
specific cup size could've. "Well, anyway, one day she came into
work wit' the sweetest smell, attitude and a skirt 'dat showed off 'dat
a...," with that he was shot to his feet by sheer ecstasy! He stuck his
butt out like a rooster. He again caught himself just as his mouth got
ready to say the A word and then he again said, "Woo wee!" I got the
picture. "So later 'dat night I saw her at the Purple Palace." The Purple
Palace was a local dive that was a fish bowl of disease. People hung
out there, got drunk, had fights, got thrown out, went home and came
back the next day to do it all again. "It wasn't the normal packed
Friday crowd, probably 'cause it was rainin'. At the end of tha'
night she axed me to give her a ride home."

"All night she was akin like she wanted me to feed her kitten."
He laughed to himself and said, "Someday you'll understand."
He was right, but on that day all I could think of were the stray
feline ghetto beasts around our block that looked more like
mountain lions than cats. National Geographic camera men would
have freaked if they had been called on assignment to capture
these prehistoric missing links. They were bigger than most small

dogs and mean as shit. I thought that my father would have to have been a brave man to have provided such a service as feeding one of these killers under any conditions, rain or otherwise. This time, thinking I knew what he was talking about, not only did I give him a nod, I smiled and as if to say, 'Yeah, daddy, I know what you're saying.'

"Tha' end result was that 'dat night at her pad I made a decision and somethin' serious went down 'dat will always affect me, regardless of if ya' mother ever finds out."

"What happened dad?" These were the first words I'd spoken all morning. They came out raspy because I still had sleep in my throat.

"You know all you need to know fa' now. When you grow up, I'll tell you more." He knew I wouldn't tell my mother or anyone, but for some reason he felt I wasn't ready to hear the rest of the story. I trusted him that I would be better suited to hear the story when I was older. I didn't ask anymore questions. We were close like that, we had been more like friends than a father and son. This was probably because of our closeness in age. I got to watch HBO and he didn't avoid cursing around me. I had finished many a beer of his, even though it was probably more backwash than beer. I'd even taken a shot of vodka once. He'd tell me about girls, things I should and shouldn't do. Although he never really got specific, he was clear. Kids my age weren't talking to their dads like this. Probably because most didn't have fathers living with them. But I did. For much of those years I was proud of that. I liked having my father take me to my little league games and help coach my Pop Warner football team. I felt special. Not just because I had a dad, but because mine really loved me. He was strict with me, but he never got mad at me. If I did something bad, he'd tell me he was disappointed with me and if I really acted up, sure, I'd get a beating, but then it was done. I was Tarique Junior. Although I never admitted it, I loved when people called me 'Little Tarique' or told me I look just like my dad. I would spend every minute I could up under him. Fixing the car, doing repairs around the house, anything, I looked up to my dad as if he were ten feet tall. The only thing that brought him down to earth in my eyes was his propensity for physically and mentally beating my mother down.

I loved my father. I just hated what he did to my mother. I always wished he'd just stop. I guess the thought never crossed his mind. It was as if she was serving a life sentence for marrying him. My father was many things, batterer, provider, a strong man and a selfish little boy, but most of all he was the epitome of complexity. He could embody hatred. His mere presence could be so ominous that even the most beautiful day seemed, at best, bleak. Yet, he had a smile that could paint any day with the most brilliant colors.

"Ya see, I love ya' motha' and I would neva' do nothin' ta' hurt her, 'dat's what is tha' difference between me and Hi-C. Me and Jennifer get into it from time ta time, but it ain't nothin' like 'dat," he pointed to a now crying Shanna.

While my father was telling me his story Hi-C and Shanna were still going at it; pushing each other and calling one another every name they could think of. At one point they ran out of names to call each other so they put 'fuck' in front of whatever they said and a brand new list of insults were born. Bitch became "Fuckin' bitch". The versatility of the F-word prolonged their argument at first, but hatred overtook linguistic acrobatics, leaving a fight. Once they started fighting my father stopped telling his story and turned into Howard Cosell.

"Look at 'dat mess," he commanded, and so I did. "Dat joker is kickin' her ass. He looks like he is goin' to beat her from now on. 'Dat shit ain't right...OOH!" He scrunched up his face and put his hands on top of his head as if he were blocking an imaginary blow to his head. "You see 'dat?!," he yelled. My father's questions were coming as frenzied as the blows that Shanna's almost lifeless body was absorbing. She was up against the car that they were getting into before the fight. Like Shanna, I had to let them come.

"OOH SHIT! He just kicked her!" Shanna was pregnant. No longer fighting back, she cowered in pain. Her fight was now for her life and the life of her baby. The look of helplessness in her swollen eyes was all too familiar to me, but I guess my father never got a chance to notice it. Just like when he beat my mother he was consumed with the fight itself. Never once, not when he was doing it or as he watched Hi-C do it, did he ever realize that there was a person at the end of those fists. In both cases he was too concerned about the fight.

"AWW MAN!," my father exclaimed as he saw Hi-C, out of breath and bent over with his hands on his knees, take the last bit of energy he could muster to spit on Lashana's limp body. "He didn't even have to do 'dat," my father said with disgust. The whole incident lasted no more than 15 seconds. Time never moves as slowly as when it is submerged in pain.

Shortly after watching Hi-C 'take care of business,' my father started telling me what it was to be a black man in our society. He was feeling especially philosophical and I didn't have the heart or guts to tell him that he was talking my ears off, so I started to sweep again. To him, black men had every right to act out their aggression any way they needed because of the hardships they'd suffered. But he also felt that sooner or later black men had to get themselves together and stand up and be men. He'd always talk about how black women had helped create this atmosphere of dependency, first as mothers and then as mates.

"Tha' reason Hi-C ain't had no job is 'cause Shanna lets 'dat lazy nigga sit up in her house, eat all tha' Frosted Flakes and drink up all tha' red Kool Aid, and you know how mad niggaz git when 'dey git 'dey mouf ready and git to tha' 'frigerator and ain't no mo' Kool Aid lef', 'specially when it's hot as hell like 'dis." My lesson in life continued, "Now, Hi-C got all 'da booty he wants and mo' Kool Aid 'dan one man can drank. Why in tha' hell is he gonna get a job fo?" I again shrugged my shoulders to move along the story and again it worked.

"See too many nigga's say 'dat 'dey castrated by 'da System, but really 'da system gave 'em a lobotomy. It ain't took away their nuts, it took away their brains. 'Dey think that sellin' drugs is gonna get 'em somewhere, but it ain't gonna do nothin' but get 'em a nice car and a TV for their roach infested apartment in the projects. In tha' end the Man is gonna come and take all that shit and them too. If 'dey went to college and got a job like me 'dey wouldn't have to do 'dat mess." To some extent I guess he was right. He never missed a day of work and we never wanted for a dime. He owned his own home and both he and my mother had a car. Although he went to a trade school, not a college, he did further his education in an attempt to make his life better.

Shortly after Hi-C left the police came and Shanna was taken to the hospital. She miscarried.

After the fight and Philosophy 101 ended, my father and I went in the house to get the measurements for a new window. Although he'd spent more time talking than anything, I was able to get a good amount of the sidewalk cleaned up. My mother had lunch ready when we got in. By that time it was almost 1:30 in the afternoon. My father and I sat in front of the broken window and ate our lunch. He was still talking, I continued to provide the occasional shrugs and nods as needed, and so flowed the conversation. As he talked I noticed how much easier it was to see out of the broken window. I said this to him and he said, "Yeah, it's easier ta' see what everybody else is doin', but it's much mo' dangerous ta' look out of a broken window." He went on to say that looking out of a broken window deprives us of the reflection of ourselves that comes from a full window. "It's us that we need to be lookin' at, not other people. If more people minded their damn business and took care of 'dey stuff firs', 'den more shit would be right in this world."

We put a piece of cardboard in the window for the night. Early that Sunday morning my father went to get a replacement window. While he was gone my mother packed a trash bag. She didn't have to say much to me, just, "You know I have to do this?" To which I sheepishly nodded 'yes'.

She told me to go in my room to get Teddy. I could taste my heart beating in my throat. My father said before he left that he'd be right back, which translates into 'I'll be gone for ten minutes'. He was never late. He gave us both specific instructions to be there when he got back.

His words didn't scare my mother that Sunday. She was determined to live. I had seen death in her eyes for so long that I'd began to think that that was what she looked like. So when life started to shine through her swollen face, I was called to action. At first I felt like I couldn't run fast enough, I couldn't follow her closely enough, I knew he was on his way home, I could smell it, but life had kicked on the generators and life was crying out from every hurried movement she and I made.

"Tarique," she patiently called to me as if dinner was on the table. No, my mother wasn't afraid anymore. But I was, oh boy was I. My father had just gone up the street. I could see the store from my bedroom window. I wanted the beatings to stop. I wanted my mother to live, I wanted to obey her, but I couldn't. I knew that if we left, if she took his son, he would kill her. So I took my time, hoping he'd hurry home and she and I could act like nothing happened. "Tarique, hon'…"

"I'm coming mom." But I wasn't. I was sitting on my bed. I had never seen her this way. She was so alive. The cage in her mind had been opened. She had flown around her imagination many times so she knew that she could fly. All doubt and fear were gone, all that stood in her way was opportunity.

"Tarique baby, we've got to get going."

"Okay mom, I'll be down in a second." I sat on my bed, hugging Teddy, frozen with fear.

The door opened, "Tarique, really, we've got to go." My mother had come into my room. As she stood in the doorway her self-esteem wrestled the pain to help her stand erect. The rush of life and the hope that it brought filled the room with the smells of spring. She was empowered and that was all I needed. I was ready to follow her wherever she was going to go.

I stood up, looked around, grabbed my mother's extended hand and we ran as fast as we could down the stairs to the front door. When I reached to open the front door, "Wait," she said.

"But mom…," I pled.

"Tarique, I'll be right back. Everything will be all right." My heart was beating so hard that I could hear it in my ears now. My mother rushed back into the bedroom. I heard drawers open and close. Time stood still as I waited at the front door. 'Please mom, hurry', I thought, but all that happened were more drawers opened and closed. 'Oh, God, please..', more drawers. Then, out of nowhere, "Tarique, are you okay?"

"Ya, ya, yes mom."

"Let's go then." With a garbage bag in one hand and a picture of my father and me at the Wildwood Amusement Park in Jersey in the other, we left. We ran down the block to catch up to a departing SEPTA bus. It felt like everyone was looking at us, my mother, with her bruised face and wig shifted to one side, said nothing. She looked forward and smiled defiantly.

We spent the next three weeks in the Salvation Army's battered women's shelter. Within a month we spent our first night alone in our new apartment in the Mantua Housing Projects. The world had stopped spinning for a moment, giving us just enough time to get off. Although I never asked her why, my mother told me that she couldn't take it anymore and there was no more room for apologies. She said nothing could ever erase what he'd done to us.

Daddy, I guess you were right, you never can get all of the glass out of the sidewalk.

Steve Perry

The Meeting
Chapter 2

That night was the first time that she laid with him. He was reddish-brown, erect and throbbing with the potential for life. Those residing within him swelled him with burning anticipation as they feverishly readied themselves to travel his urine stained veins for a race towards the light shining through his single opening.

We didn't have to live in the Mantua Housing Projects long for me to see that they were latent with contradiction and tragedy. It was a dream factory, a cracked house. It was ten stories of aesthetically smooth brick, tactilely coarse. It was a playground with no swings, a basketball court with bent rims and no nets. It was surrounded by a three-foot high fence, riddled with gaping holes. Its residents were choked by the outside world's exaggerated concept of addicts and welfare queens, suffering from some of its painful accuracy. It was mothers slightly beyond a decade older than their children, attempting to be grown-ups. It was a six year old who couldn't spell his own first name, but who could shoot a basketball with the accuracy of Dr. J. and tell you which rolling papers are the best. It was where only the strong survived and survival was relative.

From our 7th floor windows we could see the Philadelphia skyline. Its silhouetted structures looked like glowing tombstones. Its lights beckoned lost souls to its cement shores and its streets laying scars on the earth's gentle skin, demarcating paths too often traveled.

We moved there in the summer of 1980. The music of Rick

James and a strange sense of pride, which said that you've got to protect your piece of nothing, because it is worth everything, clouded the vision of some of our project's residents. This was the place where Super Fly came years before and he stayed long enough to hook up with a Super Freak and together they've danced to the Rhythm of the Night. She has made him feel good and he left as the music played on. In 1980 Papa was still a rollin' stone and he left too many sisters all alone.

My mother knew everybody who lived there, but she never expected to share their graffiti and trash filled stairwells. Nor did she expect green water stains on her sink. She never dreamed of having a heating system that didn't let the temperature drop below eighty-six degrees where she lived. For my mother and me, this place was prison with rent, a home without a welcome mat.

When she stood in the doorway to her new bedroom that first morning, even her still blackened eyes couldn't hide the despair that comes from staring into the abyss that is the unknown. All she knew was what had been and that she didn't know what to expect. Her plan was to flee, and she did, but what now? What was the next step? It is said that a journey of a million miles begins with the first step. She'd taken that first step, but she had no idea which direction she should take. Fear was her inspiration for leaving and now fear had frozen her in her tracks. She didn't know what would become of her life or her child's. A single parent? Raising a boy? Living in the projects. Everything she'd come to know was changing. She'd entered into one of the most uncomfortable stages in life, transition.

Transition for my mother was a winding bumpy road that leads nowhere. Each turn was yet another introduction into the unknown. It was a highway without signs and no one could tell her how to get there from here. Experience on its paths of irony only breeds more confusion. Transition was dusk; where night and day, life and death meet. It was here where the uncertainty of a new season of our lives was met with both anxiety and optimism. So she ended where she began, standing in the doorway to her new bedroom in transition. The road to the other side of transition was paved with the pain of not knowing. Uncertainty was the only thing she could be sure of. In transition her questions gave birth to other questions and answers lay dormant. Lost was the sure footing of knowing, found was the uncertainty of dusk. For at dusk, only time could tell if she had had a wonderful day or a difficult night.

The Saturday morning ritual with my father was old hat. Now she had to figure out how to work the 'damn shower'. Nothing tastes good when it is shoved down your throat. My father's lunacy had forced my mother's mouth open and slammed the Mantua Housing Projects in so deep that it scraped her tonsils before settling in the pit of her stomach. My mother was 26 when we left my father. She was 16 and unmarried when she got pregnant with me. Abortion wasn't an option back then, but it was a living breathing thought. She was scared and she felt sort of stupid. How could she have allowed this to happen? What was she thinking. Sex, before marriage? It was the sixties, but she thought she was old fashioned.

She had entered motherhood a girl and left marriage still a girl. She stopped being Jennifer at 16. She was Tarique's mother or Tarique's wife. Sandwiched between motherhood and a constant pursuit of marital bliss, her development as her own woman was stunted. She took no time to be her, whoever 'her' was. She was lost in her own soul, tangled in her desires to be the best mother and wife, struggling to eek an existence of her own. Was she weak, docile? Some could say, but they'd be wrong. She was just committed, strong in a way that she ended up being hurt by her own strength. It worked against her. She believed beyond that which she saw and felt. She had faith, pure and potent. She had forgiveness, willingly giving up the other bruised cheek. My mother wanted it to work and, in her mind, if she had to die many deaths trying, then she would die triumphantly. She didn't consider failure as an option. She was married and a mother. Those where two commitments for life. Sure nobody else was staying or even getting married, but she was her and they were them. Jennifer got married and, like her mother, was going to stay married. Her marriage was socially imposed, but she believed in the vows she'd taken.

For a long time I thought my mother was a saint. When so

many people in my life were doing something wrong, I saw her as a glittering oasis in a sea of pestilence. She was extremely uncomfortable with my characterization of her. She knew that she was human and a woman. I'm not sure if she knew what this meant beyond the fact that she knew that she wasn't perfect. She told me that, "Everybody has done somethin' wrong and everybody is still doing somethin' wrong." According to her, the best thing any human can be is humane. "Nobody's perfect Tarique. Anybody tells you that they're perfect is a perfect example of a liar. I did plenty of things I'm ashamed of or wish I could take back, but I can't, 'cause life ain't like that." She would try to get me comfortable with being me. "Don't worry 'bout otha' people, 'dey have they're own stuff to handle."

"Everybody's got skeletons in 'dey closet and some people got a whole graveyard, but all that means is that everybody makes mistakes." I don't think I ever really accepted, what I saw as, her modesty. To me, she was perfect, beautiful in every way. I never told her that, but I think she knew. Although I tried, I couldn't get her to agree that she was perfect. One thing we both agreed on though, was that the projects were not the place for her.

We'd been in apartment 721 for a little over eighteen hours. The little bit she was able to get together before he got home was in that trash bag. The counselors at the shelter eventually got us some paper plates and a few dishes. They were nice enough to wrap them up with newspaper and then pack it all in a few boxes. We also got some canned goods and bricks of government cheese. I got a few shirts, but mostly underwear. They gave my mother some outfits for work. She looked really pretty in them. I know that she hated them, but I thought she looked like a model. One counselor had been through the same thing. My mother really connected with her. Paula Marino, she was Italian.

Shortly after we got to the shelter, Ms. Paula went to the drug store and got my mother some make-up. It was the wrong color, too light. Paula was sweet, but white. She and my mother laughed about the make-up thing. My mother appreciated the thought. It was the first time I'd seen her laugh in a long time. She would not have made it through those first few weeks without Ms. Paula. On those nights when my mother was doubting her decision and considering going back to my father, it was Ms. Paula who stayed long after her shift had ended to console her. Ms. Paula knew where she was coming from, she had two young daughters when she left her husband. All three had stayed at the shelter until she could get on her feet. That was how she became a counselor. By trade she was an attorney. She mostly did contracts for the trucking industry. But as she spent more time in the Salvation Army shelter she began to see a way for her to help others while helping herself. So she began to volunteer. She'd draw up the divorce papers, file restraining orders and other stuff like that. She also led women's groups. That's how she and my mom met. After group they'd talk for hours and when Ms. Paula could sense that my mother was wavering, she'd even spend the night. All the people there did all they could to help. Everybody knew that it was going to be difficult for my mother and so they gave all that they could to build her up. They also knew that in the end she'd have to live with her decisions. So they tried their best to give us some things to make our new place a home, but this place was just where we were living, it wasn't home.

My mother's lost feet made a bizarre sound as they slowly trudged across the gritty linoleum kitchen floor outside her bedroom. She was lost in this empty box with sweating walls. Sitting in my room, I heard her fumbling through the cabinets as she tried to remember where she put the 'damn cups'.

This just wasn't her house. Her house had a basement, a second floor and just enough yard to put a grill in it on Labor Day. Her house wasn't a palace, but it had a kitchen floor with eight years of wax build-up and a table that had hosted some of the most intense Spades and Pokeno games ever played. Her living room was draped in more velvet than a 70's pimp. On the wood paneled walls there were black velvet pictures of a woman and man with afros. Her living room set was velvet too. Crushed red and black paisley velvet, to be exact, with plastic seat covers. The plastic was there to protect the couch. The plastic also served the purpose of sticking to your skin when you sat on it with shorts. It also reminded you that you were sitting on something of value.

The bedroom in the place that, just a month before, she called home, was decked out in orange and it had zodiac signs with people in all kinds of sexual positions on the walls. She and her husband decorated it. The rest of the rooms were symbolically protected by colorful plastic or brown, wooden beads hanging in the doorway. The air in that house was filled with the smell of big dinners and incense. Her house had a stereo with an eight track player, a husband and a son, a family.

This place where she now lived had bars on the windows. There were no stairs in it because you couldn't go up. Her kitchen was empty, except for the plastic cups from the shelter. The cement walls in her living room were painted a pale blue/green. There were no paintings or livingroom set. Her bedroom was hers alone. Except for the picture she brought with her of my father and me at the Wildwood, it was empty. Wooden doors separated rooms and the metal front door lead to a hallway, not a front stoop. There were no meals on the stove. The repugnant odor of other people's heated, green, hair grease, a healthy dose of piss and mildew snuck through the window in her room. She couldn't ward off the stench.

There was no evidence of a family there. Our house on 36th and Mount Vernon was special, not because of the baby pictures that hid scars on the walls administered by rage, but simply because it was ours. Apartment 721 belonged to the Philadelphia Housing Authority. Any time PHA said that you could only play Devotion but so loud, then, unless you had a pair of those big Martian headphones, then Philip Bailey's falsetto had to be confined to a whisper.

Nothing was HERS anymore, not like before. The stairs that led to our apartment, led to six more on that same floor. If our heat was out, then we could bet the whole floor's teeth were chattering. There were two people above and below us, as well as one on each side, and let's not forget all of the people across the hall.

My mother had always pretty much kept to herself. Her life revolved around my father and me. She had a few girlfriends but that was it. She barely kept in touch with them, because my father was very jealous. He wanted to know where she was all of the time and he hated when her friends called. He'd say, "Them bitches always callin' here tryin' to interfere and mess up our lives. If 'dey had their own life, 'dey wouldn't be callin' here!"

That first morning in apartment 721 was very difficult for my mother. She was dealing with the cutting feelings of failure, uncertainty and resentment. She was afraid that she'd let me down by taking me away from my father. She knew that I'd loved him and she didn't know how I'd feel about leaving. But at the same time she was mad as hell at him for causing all of this.

After a few minutes of lying in my room on the blankets that my mother had put together so I wouldn't have to sleep on the cold floor, I came into the kitchen. We talked for a few seconds. Her left eye still had a red scar from my father's wedding ring. The shame of calling it quits with her marriage and the potential harm that could come from trekking through this urban Siberia with her son on her back was written all over her battered face. Through her once swollen lip she swore that she'd do her best to give me a good life. She went through that first day continually apologizing and making sure that I was adjusting to the move. She made sure I understood she did this so I would never have to go through sweeping up after her and my father. She apologized endlessly for the way we moved and for me having to leave behind my friends.

I was silent as she spoke that morning. I felt awkward. I didn't know what to do with my hands or how I should stand. I'd cross my arms in front of me, then locked my fingers behind me, then shift my weight. She didn't seem to notice. She just kept vowing that she'd do whatever needed to be done to give me a good life.

I could tell that she was no more comfortable than I was. Her words skipped and curved through her mouth. When she started to sense my discomfort, I gradually slowed my movements to near paralysis. The only time I moved was to slowly nod. My eyes never moved from her face. As I peered at her I don't think that I blinked. We both knew that it was getting harder for her to hold back the tears so I stopped looking at her in hopes that that would help. This only made it worse. Within seconds she broke down. Her head dropped into her hands and then she turned away from me, put her elbows on the kitchen counter and cried as I'd never seen her cry. I can only imagine the blank stare on my wide face and wider eyes. I was stuck. My mouth was open, my chest was expanded with enough air to say something, anything. But I couldn't. There were no words. I wanted to say something. I wanted to comfort her, tell her that it was gonna be all right, that I was fine with the move, loved the new place and couldn't wait to start at the new school. I wanted her to know that she made the right decision. 'I wanted to leave,' is what I would have said, but instead I was still. Then I opened my mouth and said, "I." Nothing more came out. One word, one letter and then nothing. Where was my courage? How could I just let her cry? 'Say something!,' I thought to myself. Nothing. No words, no movement, nothing. I swallowed deep and then, frustrated, I exhaled the air that I thought I was going to need to comfort my mother.

When I looked into her troubled eyes I saw her tormented soul. I knew at that moment that there was no such thing as God, heaven or hell. If there was a God how could He have allowed this woman to suffer like this? If there were a God, He would have answered my prayers. Yet, I never got a five speed bike and my father spent more than a few days kicking my mother's ass. I had asked God to kill my father or at least put him in a lot of pain when I'd hear her gurgling for air. And what did He do? Shit! That's right, He let that bastard go on torturing her. All I ever asked of Him was that He spare my mother pain for one week, one fucking week! And He never delivered. What kind of God would do this? It seemed like the more I asked of Him the more pain He gave her. 'I hate you God!,' I said to myself. 'I hate you and your Goddamn big hat wearing fat women and their homosexual choir director husbands!' As I stood there and watched her cry, I couldn't help but question, 'Why in the hell should I do good when people like my mother do good and still get hurt? I asked You for happiness and You gave me a fucked up little life. You ain't shit God! You ain't shit.' And with that I started to cry. Then, I ran out of the kitchen and into my room. When I got there, I put my face down on the bed of blankets and punched the floor, damned God and cried some more.

After a few minutes she got herself together and yelled to me that there was no food. This meant she wanted me to go to the store. I cleared my throat, lifted my head from the blankets and answered, "OK." I realized that, more than anything, she needed some time alone. I got washed up. Then I went through the trash bag full of clothes that we got from the shelter and got dressed. When I got into the kitchen I saw that even through her saddened face shined the never dimming love that is only a mother's to give. I had never seen my mother like that. We'd become close over the years because we'd spent so much time on the emotional roller coaster that my father conducted.

It's not like he was physically kicking her ass every day. But the man just didn't respect her. Each day started with a slow assent up the massive incline. When he got home from work there was a pregnant pause. During the pause my mother and I would look at each other and brace ourselves, wondering, 'Is he in a good mood today?' Our stomachs would fill with frantically fluttering butterflies while our hearts raced. And then, on a bad day, WOOSH! We were thrown down the first hill, slammed into a turn, snatched into a twist and catapulted over a series of waves and troths. We were glued to our seats by the force of the run-a-way car. Our knuckles were white and our fingernails left indentations in the car's vinyl interior. Our screams were inaudible because we were traveling at the speed of light. Our eyes burned from the strong wind pressing our skin against our skulls like wet silk, while it pushed streams of tears across our temples. The conductor was intoxicated with adrenaline. Thrashing, dipping, climbing, our car had run amuck and then WHAM! Our bodies shot forward forcing our heads and knees to share a common space. It was over.

I knew the neighborhood so I knew where the store was. Our old house was about 10 to 15 blocks away, but as a lazy ten year old, blocks may as well have been miles. Especially since my only mode of transportation was connected to my ankles. With no bike, no money for tokens for SEPTA and no desire to walk I didn't spend much time in the projects. But I had been there a few times so I kinda knew where stuff was. On my way out my mother stopped me, grabbed my narrow shoulders between her hands, looked me in the eyes and said, "You're the man of the house now Tarique." The significance of that comment made a thud when it hit me. My mother was saying she needed me. This woman who was a perennial Gibraltar of courage, who stood tall for as long as her body would allow, now needed me. I was only ten. What could I do? Nobody had ever needed me for anything more than taking out the garbage and now I'm supposed to be THE MAN OF THE HOUSE? All the way to the store and back I thought about my new role as a MAN. It was a task I decided I was ready to take on. Or did I? I realized that if I didn't, then nobody would. With that, my decision became easy. Without much thought I literally stuck out my flat smooth chest, arched my back and prepared for manhood.

I knew that there was no listing in the *Philadelphia Inquirer* that said, "Jennifer Oakman needs a man. All Negroes are encouraged to apply." The shit was more complex than that. The last thing I wanted was some greasy nigga' with a curly kit and something to prove knocking on the door talking about, 'You betta' respect me.' Nigga' please. I knew that that shit was dead. If there was to be a man in the house, he was gonna be me or he'd have to go through me. That was for damn sure.

That night, as the rain played an unfamiliar melody on the bars outside my window, I heard my mother's muffled crying. The sounds of her crying and the drumming on my windowsill were driving me crazy. I tossed and turned until the "bed" was all balled up. All that separated me from the floor were those pajamas with the feet in them. The neighborhood below was still as the rain washed away the sounds of summer. The silence only made my mother's crying seem louder. After a while I stood up and started to walk around. As I came to my window I stopped to look at the rain. Colored silver by the streetlights, it looked and sounded like dimes falling from the sky, steadily pinging against my window.

Nothing that was going on made any sense. My young mind cramped as I tried to figure out what a man was supposed to do. Midway through the night I came to the conclusion that being a man meant being like my mother, sacrificing and parting with that which was childish. Sure this was a hell of a realization for a four foot eight inch tall, seventy-five pounder like me to tackle, but I knew I had no other choice. What was I going to do, tell my mother, 'Ya' know mom, I've considered the offer that you presented and I think I'm gonna have to pass, because there's a kickball game that's got my name on it.' I realized that responsibility had run me down like a pride of lions. It was then that I looked over at Teddy. He'd always known how to comfort me. I knew what I had to do.

After my mother stopped crying and went to sleep, I slipped into her room. I kissed Teddy, carefully laid him beside her. Then I made my way back to my room. I wasn't concerned about her waking up. She was a hard sleeper. As I went back to my room, I walked gingerly, but not for fear of waking her. My thoughtful stride had more to do with the fact that the floors were linoleum and, yes, those plastic things on the bottom of my pajamas. This was a new crib but some things never change. With those things on I could have fallen and chipped a tooth. So I walked back to my room with one hand on the wall like a drunk, reminding myself, "Heal toe, heal toe..."

For the next two days I barely left my mother's side, until, I think she got MAN OF THE HOUSED to death. I was a toy soldier strutting around "protecting" my mother from all that might come her way. I fluffed her pillows and even cooked her breakfast one morning. The dish started as eggs, but when I plopped my creation on the table, she politely crunched her way through the molten mess laced with remnants of shells. Her only comment was, "I think it needs more Lawry's."

It was on the second night of manhood that I think I went too far. My mother had come home late from her second job. In the short time that we lived there my mother was developing an after-work ritual. She'd come in and sit down on the couch she'd gotten from the Salvation Army. Then she'd take off her shoes and prop her feet up on the coffee table that I'd found in the dumpster. That was where she usually fell asleep.

As I looked at her sleeping with her mouth all open and drool making its way to her blouse, I felt that it was obvious that she needed to laugh. I thought about it for a little while. A bunch of things came to my mind. I first considered making her a late dinner, but after the breakfast incident she told me that, "Men don't cook." So cooking was out. Then I thought about playing the fart game, but the last time she caught me and my friends doing that I got a very long and painful beating. So no fart game. Then I looked over and saw her naked feet. I thought, 'This was the perfect opportunity to play 'This Little Piggy'.' It always made me laugh. How could it fail? By the time I got past the first little piggy going to the market my mother had jumped up and indefinitely relieved me of my MAN duties. I neglected to consider a few things. My mother wasn't just sleeping, she was exhausted and she wasn't ten.

First thing that next morning, she told me she didn't want me hanging around the house anymore, followed by a, "Go outside and play."

It was then that I got the feeling that she was serious about my demotion to the status of a child. I had to confirm her sudden change of heart. I asked her, "Are you sure that you don't need me?"

Her answer was the quickest in the history of spoken language, "NO!". So there I was, pushed out to the edge of the branch and told to fly. My first thought was that I needed to consult Teddy, but he was serving a different tour of duty now. I was on my own.

This new neighborhood was exactly like what I was used to and absolutely different at the same time. Our building was a bizarre sorority house with children. At first glance it appeared as if no fathers were allowed. Norman Rockwell's brush would've frayed had he tried to paint Thanksgiving Dinner in our building. Wall to wall women and their kids. Sure men came, but that was all they did. Too few of them stayed to take responsibility for their contribution to the maze of lost children. All they wanted was sex and they got a baby. Theirs was a visit of satisfaction, so when the mission was accomplished, they'd disappear. But the women let them do it. I never knew why but they just kept letting these guys come and go. I'm not sure if the men or the women even considered that someday the baby that their thoughtlessness created would become a child. To get to that level of reality must have been too damn much for horny little boys and girls with adult's organs.

These men came in and sat down at the table of satisfaction for too long. They gorged themselves and when they realized what they'd done, they regurgitated that which they didn't come for. What they left behind cried out for their guidance, but they left it there for somebody else to clean up. Unfortunately they came when they should have left. Too many of our fathers always knew what to say, but all they did was talk. There were more promised weekends to the Philadelphia Zoo and Veteran's Stadium than there was distance between those statements and reality. The person hurt most by the empty promises wasn't always us kids, who sat by the window like anxious puppies anticipating their owner's return home. It was our mothers. They had to make excuses to their teary eyed little trooper as to why it was 3:00, the game had already started, and our fathers weren't there yet and probably weren't coming.

My void of male companionship made my venture into the concrete jungle lying below our apartment even more distressing. Everybody knew we were new in the building, including the bullies. They knew that it was just me, no big brothers, no uncles, nothing. The door was open for the terrorism to begin. The summer was a double-edged sword. I didn't have to go to school which meant I didn't have to fight the whole school. But on the other hand, there was no excuse as to why I wasn't outside, 'on such a beautiful day.' Which meant I might have to fight the whole neighborhood instead. I tried to explain to my mother that I felt it was my duty to stay by her side for as long as it took for HER to adjust to her new neighborhood. In my mind I'd hoped this would take until I was about twenty years older and two hundred pounds heavier. But my mother was just not having it. She politely thanked me for the support, but she said that she could take it from there. I still had hope.

I thought to myself, there is always a bug of some sort going around somewhere. This was the perfect opportunity to capitalize on the medical profession's inability to conquer its environment and, the common cold. So it began.

The plan was to stay "sick" for as long as possible or at least until school started. That night was like the two days of nights before it, hot! The temperature, coupled with the heat going on and off, gave me the perfect climate for a FEVER! I had the whole thing planned. I'd go to bed in my clothes, keep the windows shut, then wake up before she did and open the windows. By that time it'd look like, even with the windows open, I was sweating like a nervous fat man in Bermuda. To add to the effect, I went into the kitchen and filled two cups with water and put them on my windowsill. I remember smiling before I went to sleep thinking, 'Who does she think she is telling me to go outside? I'll go outside when I'm ready.'

When I woke up the next morning I realized that in the middle of the night my mother came into my room, opened my bedroom windows and even undressed me! Apparently, with her sixth mother sense, she felt compelled to check on me as I slept. As if that wasn't enough, she brought the fan from her room and turned it on me to keep me cool! It dried every bit of sweat that might have accumulated. What was she thinking? Had she lost her mind? I started to panic. How could I have slept so hard? I frantically wondered how I would still pull off the fever bit when I was perfectly dry and room temperature? There was one last hope, the water! I reached up to the windowsill and..., they were gone! Both cups of water were gone! SHE CLEANED MY ROOM IN THE MIDDLE OF THE NIGHT! What was she an elf or some kind of fairy room cleaner? Just as I realized that my plan was foiled, I heard her coming from her room into mine. 'Oh well, I'll just have to wing it. Look out Sidney Poitier.' As she came into my room I started to moan, and Moan, and MOAN..

"What's wrong?" I told her in my best dying man's voice that I wasn't feeling well. She matter-of-factly answered, "Okay, I'll take you to Dr. Bell." I was in. Dr. Tony Bell loved me. He was a lanky dark skinned man who never smiled. Every time I went to see him he gave me candy and toys. Then he'd make me shake his hand real hard. He'd kiss my mother on the cheek and then tell her how big I'd gotten. I think he liked her, but she never paid him any mind. She'd just smile, bat her eyes and we'd be out. On our way out we'd pick up a prescription and a note that'd keep me in the house for at least a week. A week would give me enough time to think up something new to avoid the inevitable 'Let's see if the new kid can fight' scenario that awaited me in the playground below.

With the joyous news of a trip to see Dr. Bell, I had to remember to keep moaning and holding my stomach. My mother continued, "Yeah you ain't been to see Dr. Bell in a long time and, if I ain't forgot, it's time to get your shots."

"SHOTS!" I involuntarily yelled. When I realized what I'd done, I snatched both hands off my stomach and put them on my mouth. I couldn't believe it, I'd slipped out of character. But I had a right to. Was she crazy? She knew I hated shots. I'd rather be dragged behind a truck, after being run over by a stampede of crazed elephants, instead of getting a needle. I couldn't believe it. My moms was trying to sell me out! When I realized that she was serious, I jumped up and put on some clothes. I got dressed in seconds and as I flew past her my mother, her nightgown fluttered like a humming bird's wings. On my way out the door, and I yelled, "It's a miracle, I'm cured!"

I'd been dumped into the cruel world commonly known as a playground. I sat on a bench. Its green sun smoothed pain't warmed my skin through my clothes. As I sat there I tried my best not to look new. It wasn't that I'd never fought before, that was how I got lunch money on the days my mother didn't have it, or she "forgot" to give it to me. In my day I'd tossed my share of 1st, 2nd and 3rd graders. My quick temper kept me in the principal's office it also kept me in the third grade for an encore. I was in his office so much that they were thinking about putting my name under his on the door. I'd already started to get my mail there. It was my inability to walk away from a confrontation that also got me labeled with a behavioral disorder, which, they say inspired my third grade curtain call. This situation, however, was different. The kids around here had graduated from the principal's office. Some of them had been suspended. That was a place that even I hadn't been, and didn't want to go. It meant that you were so bad that there was no punishment within the walls of the school or in the minds of our teachers that could adequately cover the offense.

It didn't take long for the sharks to smell my fresh blood. There were three assigned to the welcoming committee. As they approached I could hear the theme from Jaws, dunnun, dunnun... The first one was a bony light skinned kid with teeth that stuck out like a bottle cap opener. The second was a little taller than me and he had a Jheri Curl that was dried up like October leaves. To make his "do" look even more jacked up, the chemicals in his kit had eaten his hair out in the back. It looked nasty. The last one was a fat black kid with fangs like Dracula.

The bony one was the first to speak. He talked slow, like he'd been kicked in the head. "Wa'... shooo... name?"

To show him I wasn't the least bit scarred, I looked at him for a second like he stunk before I said, "Tarique."

They all laughed, bouncing around hitting each other. Over the laughter one of them said, "What kind of dumb name is that? You Moslem or somethin'?"

I stared at them for a second, squinted my eyes like Bill Jack and said, "Ain't a damn thing funny 'bout my name." The kid with the messed up Jheri Curl, said, "Ooh, so you gotta little attitude? You mus' wanna' fight."

I shrugged my shoulders and said, "It's up to you." I was in a situation I didn't want to be in. There were three of them, and although I felt I could take the two who'd been talking, I wasn't sure about the big one.

The bony kid answered immediately, "So... you... mus'... think.. you... can...beat...all...three...of....us." I wasn't thinking that. No, no, not that. There was a lot going through my mind, but beating up all three of them, well, it never was a thought. As a matter of fact I knew I couldn't beat all of them. I really didn't even want to fight anybody. Play basketball, ride bikes, yeah, those sounded good, but fight three project kids, not at the top of my list of ways to start the day. Shoot, if I had my way, I'd have been upstairs hanging out with my mother. Those things weren't options. I had to fight, it was just a matter of who and how. It didn't matter what I wanted, with each second that elapsed between his question and my answer only helped things get further out of hand.

What could I do? Walk away? Yeah right, then I'd be called every kind of punk they could think of, beaten up on a regular and otherwise banished to the nerds pool of the playground. Make a joke? I was too nervous to make anything more than something in my pants. But I did have to find a way to avoid the beat down that felt like it was only seconds away.

So I answered, "I might not be able to beat all three of y'all but I know that if you bring yo' bony ass over here, I'll snap you in half." Then I told the one with the Jheri Curl, "and if you bring that dry ass curly kit over here I'll snatch off the rest of ya' hair that ain't burnt out." A smart mouth was not something I lacked, especially when I was scared out of my mind. This was just such a time.

My plan was either to make them laugh or to divide them so only one of them would be mad enough to fight me.

Then, like a fight promoter, "You... ain't... say... nothin'.... 'bout... my... boy... Sha Sha," the bony one pointed to the fat kid, "you... mus'... be... scared... 'a... him... " With that the two idiots laughed and yelled in unison, "YEAH, you mus' be scared."

I would've said something about the big one too because there was so much to make fun of, but they interrupted me before I got a chance. This put me in a situation. It was becoming clear that the only one there I didn't want to fight, I was going to have to fight. When I realized this I stood up from the bench and said, "I ain't scared of nobody!"

The line was drawn in the sand box. There was no turning back now. If I lost, this could be the first fight of many. Anybody who wanted to pick a fight with somebody would look for me. My reputation for having dukes would be done. If I won, the playground would become known as the place where the new kid beat up the big kid.

I was face to face with "Sha Sha," or whatever they said his name was. We looked at each other, not quite staring or glaring, just looking, curious I suppose. Thinking, maybe wondering what is was that we were supposed to do, trying to figure out how we got there. We were about the same height. He weighed more than me but I wasn't that much smaller than him. We were both pretty big kids. As we looked at each other it became clear that there were no more words to be said. Nothing more to do but, get ready for the inevitable.

My heart raced as we stood there. My hands dangled by my side. I slowly clenched my fingers in and out, flexing them in preparation for battle. It was hard for me to breath. The thick full air clogged my throat. Everything was still enough to hear the grass growing. Not even the wind dare vibrate my eardrums. We were two gladiators thrust into the playground forced to do battle. I looked into his eyes and I saw my foe. We stood in silence waiting for the cages to be opened. There was nothing between us and fate. This thing had gotten out of our hands.

We were surrounded by the trappings of childhood, swings, monkey bars, a sand box, a few bikes, you know, kids stuff. Everything we needed to create memories, have fun and escape into the porthole that lead to youthful bliss. It was all ours. Childhood, it was ours.

When I got ready to fight someone, a surge of simmering blood would rush through me. This time was no exception. My heart was thunderously beating orders to my hands. Their response was to clinch in and out faster and faster. With each new order the rest of my body readied for battle. My face got tense, my chest became hardened armor, and the hairs on my back frantically stood at attention awaiting their next command!

"Wha'...chu'...guys...gonna...do...fight..o'...kiss?"

The kid with the messed up hair answered, "Yeah, I think dey mus' like each other!" and then both of them started singing, "Sha Sha and the New Kid up in the tree, K-I-S-S-I-N-G. First comes love, then comes marriage, then comes Sha Sha in a baby carriage..."

"C'mon, you girls. Fight! What are you scared or somethin'?," Jheri Curl yelled. That was the question that made everybody fight. When you think about it, what are your response options? 'Ya' know, I actually am a little scared, I'm glad you asked.' Not in a million years! We were little boys with every thing to prove and nothing to lose. The only answer to that question was a blow to the head, or even a 'kick where it counts.' That's why I took everything I had and swung. It made no sense to me to let this big black joker hop on me before I did my best Muhammad Ali dance routine. 'Bob and weave, bob and weave,' I kept reminding myself.

My blow connected. But somehow I only managed to hit his shoulder! I couldn't believe it, his shoulder?! There we were, at a stand off, we took ten paces, turned, shot, and the best I came up with was a shot to the shoulder! I thought, 'My God. I'm dead.'

Sha Sha hit me with a right hook and I saw my life reel in front of me. When it connected it dimmed the lights in my mind's movie theater. When it landed on my chin I went stumbling down the rows until I found my seat. Flesh-seeking fists exploded on the screen in the July of my life, each toppling its intended target. The site of their destructive force, ripping through skin like a comet, brought my father to the screen. The deeper I journeyed into my memory the more clearly I could see that my father stood behind the ghastly images. Soon we were face to face. I looked into his muddy eyes. Inaudible words exploded around me, but his eyes were the only things I could hear. Slowly I panned down his chocolate face, I glided over the slope of his forehead, whisked down his nose and dripped onto his lips where I ignited his mouth, "Are you gonna be a man or jus' look like one?!" it rang. CRASH! I hit that green park bench. The shock made me regain consciousness. I immediately bounced to my feet swinging. I connected a few times and then we locked up. I held on to him so tightly that it looked like we were attached. All the while Opey and Dopey were screaming things like, "You... guys... fight... like... girls," and ,"C'mon sissies, hit somebody!"

I don't know how it happened but we'd wrestled each other to the ground. When we got there we rolled around back and forth, struggling to get a clean shot. We must've rolled around, squirming and kicking for almost five minutes until we were both breathing as hard as our young lungs would allow. We steadily slowed in the squelching summer heat. And then we stopped. We'd fought to exhaustion. There we lay, with nothing more in common than we were both victims of a situation that had gotten out of control. Two foes whose blood ran on the pavement in harmony. Both hurt badly hurt and both vanquished.

Rocks and dirt stuck to our backs while the sun beamed rays of light that pain'ted our skin's pores into contracting. We lied there panting, cracked remnants of who we were, a memorial to control lost, contemplating who we'd become. We were trying to prove something and ended up with nothing. As our hearts' palpitations slowed, the jeers of those two buffoons became louder. They had never stopped verbally assaulting us with every insult imaginable that would question our possession of testosterone, but the last time we heard them was when this whole thing got started. Soon their foolish words were ringing in our ears again. And then, without saying a word, Sha Sha and I looked at each other. This person who'd never said anything more to me than a grunt, said, "Let's get 'em."

We jumped to our feet and took off after them. They looked at us, looked at each other and then took off screaming. We were rejuvenated. Bony went one way, Jheri Curl went the other, and we went after them. It didn't take long for me to catch the Jheri Curl kid, but Bony ran zig zaging with his arms flailing, screaming "Helllp!!!", as if death itself was chasing him. A couple of seconds later, Bony's screaming stopped. I heard a yelp and what sounded like a hundred knuckles cracking at once. Sha Sha had pounced on him. He dragged the pleading fool over to me by the throat, like he was carrying a suitcase.

I had the Jheri Curl kid pinned on the ground, he was crying. He tried everything to get up, "C'mon man, my mother is calling me...I can't breath...." When that didn't work he told me that, "'Dese are my school clothes and I can't get 'em dirty." The funniest one was, "See man, you done messed up my hair."

Sha Sha was out of breath when he got to me. While he caught his breath I sat on Jheri's chest and had fun. I'd made up my mind that I was going to torture him. I thought of just smacking him until I got tired, I decided against it. However, I did put all I had into one good one. When I connected his head shot to the left and after a few seconds I saw my hand print in the form of a welt on his right cheek. It felt so good. Jheri cried like a baby and I was getting sick of it. I told him that if he didn't stop squirming and crying I'd spit in his face. I don't know why I thought of spitting in his face but why not? He wouldn't listen. He kept begging and trying to get up so I got together all of the mucous I could gather from the back of my throat and spit two bugger filled wads to the left and right of his head. He couldn't move his head without rolling in my spit. It was so funny to see him forced to keep his head perfectly still as he begged. When that got old I told him if he opened his mouth to talk I'd spit in it. He immediately curled his lips into his mouth, held his head still and mumbled his pleas with his mouth closed. Tears were streaming down his face and snot was running from his nose. I kept asking him, "What did you say? I can't understand you," and just as he'd go to open his mouth, I'd load up my mouth to fill his mouth with flem. It was so funny.

Sha Sha caught his breath and Bony did his best to squeeze a few words from between his huge fingers. Sha Sha asked them both, "Now who's the sissy? Who can't fight?"

They both answered repeatedly, " Nobody!" Bony's answer was a little more difficult to understand because Sha Sha still had him by the throat. Jheri Curl's words weren't any easier to understand, "momoby, momoby."

Sha Sha said, "That's the wrong answer, y'all suppose to say that y'all is the sissies."

A quicker answer could not have come, "We are, we are the sissies!!!"

"Then kiss!" Sha Sha demanded.

"WHAT!" They both turned white and then Jheri remembered what I told him I'd do if he opened his mouth. He immediately folded his lips back into his mouth and mumbled the rest of his objections. I hadn't thought of this, but I respected the big kid's ingenuity. They'd been calling us girl names all day and they were the ones most resembling the Eves of this garden. What better way to prove our point than a kiss?

"WHAT!," they again resoundingly said, even Bony answered at a deafening pitch. Jheri caught himself again and closed his mouth.

"Mlease...," Jheri squeezed through his clinched mouth. I looked at him as if to say 'don't you say a word.' "Mmm mmm," he mumbled, assuring me, as he slightly shook his head, that he wouldn't say anything else.

"C'mon...y'all,...we...was...jus'...playin',...y'all...knew...we...was..jus'... playin',...right?" The "right" was thrown in as a last ditch effort to connect with a Sha Sha run amuck.

Sha Sha shrugged his shoulders and said matter-of-factly, "Well, I ain't playin'," Sha Sha had more maneuverability with Bony so he brought him over to where me and Jheri Curl were. When he got to us, he told me to, "Look out." I moved and he put Bony on top of Jheri prone. Then he put his hand behind Bony's head and pushed his skinny face into Jheri Curl's. They were both crying. Bony threatened to tell his mother. Like we cared. We would've told her.

With Bony on Jheri, Sha Sha sat on top of both of them and they couldn't move. It was perfect. I was free to hold both of their heads still. They whimpered, begged, and pleaded to be let up. Sha Sha told them to pucker their lips, they didn't so I smacked Bony as hard as I could. It felt so good to see them crying and to know that I was responsible for it.

As they cried Sha Sha yelled, "you better pucker up your Goddamn lips and get ready to kiss each otha' or else!" That 'or else' seemed to be the incentive they needed. Out went their lips. Sha Sha pushed on the back of Bony's head and said, "Walla, a match made in heaven!" He held their heads there for about 10 seconds while we laughed from the bottom of our toes. While Sha Sha was playing Chuck Woolery from the "Love Connection" I sang, "Bony and Jheri Curl up in the tree, K-I-S-S-I-N-G. First comes love, then comes marriage, then comes Bony in a baby carriage....."

When Sha Sha let them go they ran away crying and spitting. While they ran home I heard Bony accuse Jheri of trying to stick his tongue into his mouth! "No I didn't, you did!" Then Jheri Curl pushed Bony to the ground.

Bony got up and he ran off screaming, "I... gonna'... tell... my...

mother... on... you... too."

We sat on the bench and laughed as if we'd been best friends all of our lives. We rolled around poking each other. 'You so crazy, ' then I'd say, 'Naw man you crazy.'

We started talking after a while and we found out that we lived in the same building. He lived upstairs from me in 821. We were practically neighbors. We were on that bench until it started getting dark. The streetlights were about to come on, which meant we both had to go in. On the way back to our building Sha Sha said, "You know I won that fight, tha's why I let you up?"

"You crazy! As big as you is, you still couldn't do nothin' wit' me." Then we both started laughing again. We were at an age when the amount of blood extracted from your opponent's body was the barometer of victory. As we went back and forth I spotted a small amount of blood on his shirt. I put my finger on his chest where blood had dried and said, "See, tha's why you bleedin'."

"Tha's your blood, because look at your shirt," he quickly answered. I looked down and saw the spot in question and thought to myself, could he be right? Had my skin betrayed me and given way under the pressure of battle? It couldn't be.

I let him know how insane that was, "You've lost your damn mind, this is your blood and there is no need to deny it!" The rest of the way home went like this. We laughed and went back and forth as we left the sight of our meeting and headed upstairs. When we got to the door I screamed, "Oh my God, I got grass stains in my new dungarees! My mother's gonna kill me!"

There I was the victor in at least one fight, started and finished in time for dinner, and I was worried about my mother. She only had me by about an inch. For a second I thought, 'I shouldn't be worried about her, I'm as big as she is.' Then I realized that I'd momentarily lost my mind. When I came to my senses I was scared, really really scared. Sha Sha understood what it meant to have stained your new dungarees. There were some things that warranted mild anger on the part of a parent and this wasn't one of them. At a time when a kid with much more than two pair of these treasured staples of our wardrobe was seen as rich, the near destruction of a new pair was sacrilegious.

Sensing my despair Sha Sha told me to calm down. This was not a calm down of, 'Oh you silly goose, you have nothing to worry about,' it was a, 'Let's think of something that will stop you from getting your face slapped off of your skull!' I took advantage of this calming down period, because I was frantic. We needed to think of something that would allow me to see the light of day before I turned twenty. We got to the front door of our building, ready to get on the elevator, but, as usual, it was broken. We took the stairs. This gave us enough time to think up a plan. We were willing to take our chances that it's a rare occasion when a mother will beat her child in front of company, especially 'new' company. We decided that Sha Sha would come in with me and stay until my mother cooled off or he got kicked out.

When we got to the seventh floor we looked at each other and took a deep breath. At my door we again looked at each other as if to say, 'here goes nothing.' I put the key in and twisted the knob. The door opened, silence, nothing moved, not us, not a single piece of lint. Then the words, "Tarique is that you?" were carried by my mother's voice from the back of the apartment.

"Yes. Mom." That was all I was able to squeeze out from the strangle hold of fear that captured my throat. I immediately added, "And I brought my NEW friend," stressing the new. She came out to meet Sha Sha and without looking down she used her sixth mother sense to smell the grass stain. "You stained your new dungarees," she calmly said, out of the side of her mouth, like Clint Eastwood in one of his *Dirty Harry* flicks.

The tension got thick, and then out of nowhere came, "Tarique has told me so much about you ma'am. It's a pleasure to finally meet you and have you living in our building," Sha Sha said in his best 'first time you meet someone's mother' voice.

With her teeth clenched and looking at me, my mother said to Sha Sha, "Why thank you. How sweet," in her best, 'I'm not going to kill you in front of company' voice.' Then she grunted, "Well you gotta wear 'em." It worked. Sha Sha had saved my life.

I knew from that point on we'd be friends. He didn't have to come upstairs and stand in the way of my mother's anger. He could've said, "Good luck," and gone on with his day. That meant a lot to me. We spent the rest of that summer doing everything together. Not long after our fight, I stopped calling him Sha Sha, because that was the name of my foe. Shandell Eliab was my friend. We knew everything about each other. We told each other every secret, every everything. We even built our own little fort behind our building. Wherever you found Shandell, you found Tarique and vice versa. With our striped tube socks pulled up to our knees, short shorts, sleeveless shirts and Pony's on, we ran our block.

Shandell was a little under a year younger than me. Since I stayed back, we were in the same grade. The day before school started, Shandell said we should be blood brothers. He said that being blood brothers meant that we'd be friends forever and nothing could break us apart. To perform this sacred procedure we went into my mother's sewing box and got a sewing needle and he got a lighter from his mother's pocket book. We took both of them down to the fort. We made some vows like, 'If anybody messes wit' 'chu I got your back.' We burned the needle at the end. Then, one after the other we pricked our index fingers and pressed together. I still hated needles, but this was a hallowed act.

On that day our blood again ran in harmony fusing two worlds. It glistened like rubies in the early September afternoon sun, as it streamed down our fingers. There we were, together, behind our building, in our secret fort, once victims of circumstances, now captains of our destiny.

Steve Perry

Boyz, Two Men
Chapter 3

So, we searched for answers to our questions, looking for the answers. No answers, but we were taught a lesson, every day, every time. Through mistakes we learned to gather wisdom, as life's responsibility (fell) in our hands. -New Edition

We were two boys on an expedition in the Bottoms. We had no clue as to what lie ahead. Guidance would've made our journey through the days yet to be awakened, a walk in the park, but in our neighborhood even the parks glistened with the debris of the community's never-ending bout with alcoholism and drugs. Broken bottles were scattered under its trees like fallen leaves, while discarded drug paraphernalia added danger to children's games. Even with our eyes wide open we were not protected from the glare of danger.

Shandell's family life was just like a lot of other people who lived in the Mantua Housing Projects. His birth was the result of juvenile sex that left the girl with a life sentence of motherhood. The only thing that separated his parents from many other people who had sex that night was that they ended up with a baby.

Everybody calls his mother "Snooky", her real name is Sandra. Her nickname was the only thing unique about her. Snooky's story was identical to other single women in our public housing sorority house. If you made a mistake and told her story with somebody else's name, the story wouldn't need any specific alterations. Either she thought he loved her or she loved him, or no, maybe she just wanted to have a baby for him, or wait, she

63

wanted somebody to love or somebody to love her, no no, maybe he convinced her that they were making love or she probably convinced herself that sex and love had nothing to do with each other, none the less, a baby was going to be born and, for the next twenty years, two irresponsible people would need to be responsible.

I saw pictures of Snooky when she was younger. I suppose, back then, on a stormy night, she might be a good catch. By the time I met her though, she looked like the ugly sister of Flip Wilson's Geraldine. She'd spent most of her life filling her body with the toxins that kept our building's eyes red and its heart full of rage. Snooky wasn't much older than my mother but her fast living was the expressway to her looking so old. I don't know much else about her past and I didn't need to in order to get the full picture. The wrinkles on her young face were a road map of her numerous 'trips' out of reality.

When Shandell and I first started hanging out together in elementary school I had to wake up very early. My mother worked at McDonalds and would have to open by 5:30 a.m. She made me get up and get dressed when she did. We didn't have to be to school until after 8:00. To pass the time I'd go upstairs to Shandell's to wait for him to get ready and watch TV. They had cable. We didn't. Snooky was usually awake when I got there. She didn't have a job, but she did have business to take care of. By the time I got there she'd have the cartoons on for me. She knew I loved to watch the Transformers and He-Man. They didn't have much furniture, so I'd have to sit in one of those gray folding chairs. There were only two chairs in the living room. If Snooky stayed in the living room she'd be sitting on the park bench talking on the phone. I didn't care, both the cable and the TV worked, so I would've sat on the floor. Snooky was always pleasant. She'd say good morning, ask me did I do my homework and get on me if I said that I didn't. She seemed to really care. There were a few times when she'd make me turn off the cartoons until I finished it. I didn't like it, but what was I gonna do? If my clothes weren't ironed right, she'd make me go to Shandell's room and iron them. She'd give me a bowl of those government Cheereos, the ones in the big white box that say something like 'Cereal', and there I'd sit until Shandell got ready.

Some mornings I'd come in and she'd be firmly cupping the receiver in her hands as if it would pour through the spaces between her emaciated fingers. She wouldn't notice my clothes, check my homework or get me cereal. She'd be frantically whispering to the person on the other end. A shadow of anguish would be cast over her face as her words would hurriedly sneak through the phone's plastic mesh. Hunched on that bench she'd be pleading with somebody she called, "daddy," to, "Please bring me some candy!" Incessantly she'd beg him the entire time I was there. I didn't think much of it, especially if *Tom and Jerry* was on. Besides, my mother would always get on me for listening to grown folks' conversations. So I'd go into the kitchen, get the big white box of cereal, pour it, get some milk, and go back into the living room to wait for Shandell.

On mornings like those I could feel that Snooky didn't even recognize me. She'd be so focused on the conversation that the only times she'd stop begging him were when she had to catch her breath or remind him that, "You know I'll give you somethin' too, don't I always?" Over the years I found out who Daddy really was and, based on the candy he sold, nobody would mistake him for Willie Wonka. O.D.'s candy wasn't laced with sugar and if you consumed it, you should hope that it only rotted your teeth. I guess most people who saw Snooky's place might question why I didn't figure out what was going on those mornings between her and O.D. And as I think back I too wonder how I could have missed that the place was carpeted with rolling paper, infested with 'roaches', and a spider bong sat on a crate in the middle of the room ready to inject its venom into its next victim. I guess I also missed that she didn't have any curtains. Her shades were the color of pus and they had so many holes in them that they looked like ripped mesh half shirts. Sometimes though, even I forget that I was ten.

Around my block a lot of people said that "age ain't nuttin but a number" and according to what I'd seen in the first few years of my life, that statement was absolutely true. By the time I was ten, I'd seen enough drug paraphernalia for hers not to stand out. My mother didn't really smoke weed and nobody else smoked around me. I rarely saw anybody do anything with the pipes, rolling papers and syringes. Yet they were always around. I'd gotten so used to seeing them that I don't remember the first time I saw them. Almost no one had as much as she did, but even fewer had nothing at all. My mother liked to drink, so there was a good amount of liquor in the cabinets. She even smoked a pack of Newport 100's a day, it wasn't often that drugs came through our steel door.

Shandell and I never talked about his father because to him he didn't exist. All he knew about his father was that he was a married man who got his mother pregnant and then stayed with his wife. If Shandell didn't want to know anything else about him, neither did I. Our relationship flourished because we avoided taboo topics. I guess that was the key to us getting so close. He knew my father beat my mother, but he never mentioned it. I knew his mother had problems with drugs and alcohol and I left that subject alone. We both knew all these things existed in our lives. Their existence was more than enough. Talking about them wasn't necessary. When we played in his apartment and his mother was asleep because she drank too much, I made no issue of it. I didn't give him any glaring looks. We played around her. Her chemically induced sleep was seen as a condition of the game. I'd whisper, "…okay, …and the first one to wake up your mother loses."

Avoidance wasn't simply a method for dealing with day-to-day life in the Bottoms, it was a condition that resulted from living in the Bottoms. There were times when nobody seemed to see anything. This made it possible for anything to happen. To see something might make people feel that they had to do something. In order to do something you might have to put your life in harm's way. The most valiant of our community leaders said they had no concern for a physical death. They'd speak on street corners, at the community centers in our schools, churches, wherever they could get a podium and somebody to listen. It seemed like folks were listening. People in the audience would say things like, "Praise the Lord," during their speeches and afterwards everybody would go up to these leaders to tell them how they agreed, and then they'd go home and talk about what so and so had on. Nobody wanted grief. Everybody was too busy with this and that. 'I got kids, ..I gotta work, I gotta go shopping,' should have been carved into the bricks of our building. People were waiting for the community to heal itself. It is much easier to close your eyes to the darkness than it is to open them to despair. It's not that the people in the Bottoms didn't care, it just cost too damn much to do so. After working a 50 hour week, only to end up still broke and black, some folks felt that they couldn't afford to pay attention.

The kids were no different. We looked past despair as if it were a friend we saw in the grocery store that we owed money. We were kids, our life revolved around playing games. We avoided dealing with the madness of our neighborhood because we were more interested in the game of life. Shandell and I made games out of everything. TV shows, bus rides, swinging on the swings, even breathing somehow became a game, "Whoever stops holding their breath first loses, ready, set, go."

When we were on the bus, we played "Contact I got that..." This was a game where we competed to point out the best car before the other person saw it or a better one. Whoever saw the best car first won. 'Contact I got that VW Bug!' would get you nothing when the other person said, 'Contact I got that Corvette.'

S.W.A.T. was our favorite show and game. That show had one of the only cool black men on TV, outside of Jimmy Walker and George Jefferson. First we picked who was going to be the cool black guy. Whoever lost was either a white guy on the show or one of the many black criminals who shucked and jived across seventies and early eighties TV. We used Shandell's closet, a messy depression in the wall in his room, as the *S.W.A.T* Headquarters. Our handguns were ink pens and rulers. Wiffle ball bats and broomsticks where our riffles. We were usually confined to "handguns" because one time when Snooky yelled for her broom, and she saw that we took it apart, she dismantled the game.

Shandell and I were an unbeatable team. We'd roll around on the floor, pop up and blow off the heads of imaginary thugs. We always fought side by side.

We loved diving off Shandell's bed playing *S.W.A.T.*, running through the halls of our building pretending to fly like *Shazaam*, and playing with my 'Rock 'em Sock 'em Robots.' When that wasn't enough, we spent most of our time casing the neighborhood for something bad to do. Beat up some kid, steal candy from one of the stores or just break something that wasn't ours. This was where we got most of our entertainment.

My mother worked from 5:30 a.m. until 5 p.m. and Snooky was always out to lunch. From the time we got home from school until my mother got home we took care of ourselves. We had to be in the house by the time my mother got home, but outside of that, we could do whatever we wanted. We knew the routine so we squeezed more evil into the two hours between when we got home from school until my mother got home than the filmmakers did in the movie the *Exorcist*. My mother wanted us in when she got home because that's when she'd start dinner and help Shandell and me with homework. When dinner was finished she'd make us get washed up. After that she'd send us upstairs to get permission from Snooky for Shandell to stay over and to get him some clothes. Snooky never objected and after a while the only reason we went upstairs was to get Shandell more clothes. For a long time Shandell and I slept in the same bed, but by high school my mother had gotten him a bed and dresser.

Crouched down on the prowl, we pounced on unsuspecting kids, wrestled them to the ground and relieved them of their valuables. Then we'd sprint back behind our building to our secret den, The Hall of Justice, and split whatever we'd taken. During the summer, if we got money, we'd go over by Penn, on 37th and Chestnut, and get water ice. No store was secure when we were on the prowl. Shandell posted the look-out and I nonchalantly walked down the aisles tipping boxes of candy into my bag or pants. It was the thrill of the hunt more than the sweet seduction of confection that got our blood pumping.

The objective was to out-smart a grown-up or to beat a person who had his eye on us the whole time. We amassed quite a stash in The Hall of Justice. Once our surplus had grown to a considerable volume we started to explore our options. Ninety percent of what we had was candy. We couldn't eat it all, there was too much.

We found that out the hard way. One day we stole a box of Snickers Bars, Baby Ruths, about 10 packages of Now or Laters, and Pixie Sticks. We ate everything. We even ate the paper that those candy dots come on.

That night my mother cooked us fried chicken, collard greens with fat back and cornbread, and she wasn't trying to hear us throwing food away. Suffice it to say that our 64 pre-dinner snacks mixed with my mother's southern cuisine was not a culinary match made in heaven. From that point on we decided to bring the candy to school and sell it. Shop was set up during morning recess and we'd sell it until the bell rang.

Once Shandell started staying with us he and I woke up for school together, argued over who'd win in a fight, Muhammad Ali or Bruce Lee on the way to school, spit on people from our bedroom window and laugh at crippled people when we got home from school. Before we went to sleep, we'd have contests to see whose farts smelled the worst. As the years passed our lives' streams ran in unison giving birth to a raging river. Together we flowed around every bend, hit every rock and eroded anything that stood in our way. Fueled with youthful vigor, our river met any new topography with reckless abandon.

With the passing of each season we shed another layer of the fur of our youth, replacing it with pimples and pubic hair. With the onset of 'teenagehood'. Shandell and I began to develop new sensations and new senses. Our entrance into puberty took us over the threshold of time when we couldn't stand the sight of girls to a place where we couldn't stop looking at them. Who knew that a girl's hair had a purpose beyond being something to pull? We never thought that a note with the words 'I think you're cute' could turn you into the object of envy. If you can remember what that did for Rudolph's self esteem, imagine what it did for ours. There wasn't a particular day when girls started to look or even smell good. I don't know where I was when they began to matter, but I was there, wherever it was.

I do remember one of our first conversations about girls. It wasn't a conversational earthquake, it was more like a shift. Usually, conversations in The Hall of Justice centered around our next great caper or our ongoing debate over who was better, the Dallas Cowboys or the Pittsburgh Steelers, of course it was the Steelers 'cause they had Lynn Swann and Terry Bradshaw, not to mention they were my favorite team. Anyway, one day Shandell came out of nowhere with, "I think Michelle likes you." In the world of thirteen year olds, there may not be a more telling description of a girl's feelings for a boy than to "like" him. I was shaken, but I kept my cool.

Without flinching I responded, "Why you think that?" I continued my facade of indifference by looking down at whatever I was doing.

"Well, Mary Ann told me that Michelle told her that she thinks you're cute." Now things were getting serious. To be liked and considered cute, the next thing was marriage according to the thirteen year olds' guide to dating. We were not encumbered by complicated emotions or angst. There was little to hamper the free flow of 'like' once 'cute' was added into the love potion. Even I knew this. Shoot, everybody knew this. It was instinctive. 'Like and cute' was all you needed. Did she have a job, does he have any kids, a college degree, ambition or sexually transmitted diseases? These would be questions for another age, another place, another generation. We just wanted to know, 'does she really like me?' That was it. No need to know if he came from a good family or had a good relationship with his mom. We just needed to know if the source of the information knew what in the hell they were talking about. Rumor or conjecture could demolish a young man's pride. Nobody wanted to find out that the whole 'liking and cute things' was all a big misunderstanding. So we had to make sure that the person telling the person who was telling us could be trusted.

To avoid getting too excited, I turned the tables on him. I guess boys get started early on disguising their feelings. Sure, I suppose telling Shandell that I was excited that she liked me and thought I was cute, couldn't kill me, but then what would I look like to him? I knew that I couldn't let him see that I actually cared about some girl or being cute. Feelings had little use in the Hall of Justice or in the life of a little boy. Yeah we knew they were there, but if emotions like excitement were linked to anything other than a sporting event, they were significantly out of place.

So I looked up and asked him, "Since when do you talk to Mary Ann?," then I made sure to look back down at what I was doing. Talking about girls was never more important than 'fort business'. I didn't know what was going on. While I found myself engaged by the topic, I couldn't help but wonder if 'girls were really invading our fortress.'

Even with little more than three sentences spoken, we'd said volumes. I couldn't believe that Shandell was asking me about some girl. There was no precedent. Not only had he never spoken of or to girls before, he really never spoke to anybody but me and my mother. He was painfully shy. Our teachers wondered if he could talk and the other kids just kept away from him because the only time they saw him saying anything was when he was taking their lunch money.

Apparently Shandell sensed my surprise and got defensive. He snapped, "We was jus' talkin' yesterday in line durin' lunch and Mary Ann told me that Michelle like you 'cause they is best friends!"

"Dag! I was jus' askin' you." I assured him. There was an awkward pause and then, "So do you like her?" He didn't want to let the question go unanswered. During the past couple of years Shandell started to outgrow his chubby exterior and his face was becoming chiseled. His skin was an even shade of sweet licorice and his eyes were the color of midnight. He was becoming a handsome young man and I think he and the girls noticed it at the same time.

"She's all 'ite I guess. She ain't neva' done much fa' me, 'cause she's kinda' thick," I finally answered. Michelle was the first one in our class to get the seventh grade equivalent of breasts. This amounted to overgrown nipples awkwardly attached to her chest. She'd started to wear a training bra, but that did nothing more than accentuate those two mini mounds of flesh that barely separated her from the boys. She was very short, I liked that. Her brown skin flowed tightly around her perfectly round little head. She had just moved to Philly from down South. She still had her accent and I really liked that too. She was real smart. A little too smart. It used to get on my nerves to see her always raising her hand in Mr. Kensel's class. He always said she was going to be a doctor. All that still didn't help me to make sense of why we were talking about girls in the first place or why it felt good to me to be "liked" by a girl.

Shandell saw her sturdy figure and premature development as a selling point and he got excited, "Tha's why you should like her man! See if you mess wit' her, 'den I could mess with Mary Ann, and you know that that girl is fresh!" Fresh. The truest measure of beauty? Cars were fresh, clothes were fresh, but a girl being 'fresh'? A girl? Fresh? To be fresh in the 80's meant that you could grow up to be 'all that in the 90's. What was happening to us?

This began our fumbling around with the creatures known as girls. We knew less about them than anything we'd encountered, but I suppose we thought that between us we'd figure out how to win at this too. Together we never lost and we didn't intend to start. There was no one to answer our questions except us. Even if there had been, we wouldn't have listened to them.

Our interests weren't the only things changing. Our bodies started to grow hair where it didn't seem necessary for hair to be. But at the same time, the hair couldn't grow fast enough. During our early teenage years the measure of our manhood was the baritone of our voice and the amount of hair we had under our arms and in our pants. Locker rooms were the court where all perpetrators of improper testosterone output were tried. After gym class, I'd seen twelve and thirteen year olds brought to tears under the stress of peer ridicule.

Donning toweled robes, pubescent judges took the bench as we all filed in after class. Once somebody was found whose pubic hair hadn't yet decided to exit its follicles, so as to start itching the organ that was, for the first twelve years, used only to pee, it was all over. They were brought before the Bench. The sentence of public ridicule was swift and merciless. Crying in these situations only made it worse on the late bloomer. The only salvation was when the metal gavel that was the bell that told us to change classes.

My mother did her best to explain the changes we were going

through by handing us a book called <u>Where Did I Come From</u>? It had cartoon pictures of naked "mommies" and "daddies" and it talked about 'penises' and 'vaginas'. This book came in handy, but that was later when I discovered that washing yourself in a fluid motion both cleaned and "refreshed". Even cartoons can do the trick when you haven't run into the real thing. As far as telling me what I was going through psychologically and socially, the book was useless.

Handing us the book was my mother's attempt at explaining the changes her sons were going through. If life were a 'Parenting Fair', her efforts would've gotten her honorable mention. I'm sure that the reason she handed us this 'Bugs Bunny's Guide to Sex' was because she felt uncomfortable about talking to us about IT. And we damn sure didn't want to talk to my mother about IT. The one time she tried to talk to us face to face about sex I pulled the 'I know, we learned about it in school, so you don't have to explain it to me' routine, and Shandell backed me up. The wind that came from her sigh of relief made our shirts flutter. When she thought we'd learned all we needed to know about sex in gym class, taught by Ms. Coolie, our bloated gym teacher, she was elated.

My physical changes created a new question with each passing day. Every morning I woke up to an erection and a new zit. I expected my penis to grow at the same rate as my face produced excess oil, it didn't. I was embarrassed and frustrated. I felt like *Teen Wolf* as I went through my metamorphosis. I wondered if Shandell or the other guys in my class had more pubic hair and a bigger penis, but I wasn't going to look. I didn't want them to think I was a fag. Being underdeveloped was one thing, but being called a fag was worse than death. I consulted my old friend the TV, but it had no answers concerning, what seemed to me to be, a tremendously undersized penis. HBO only showed breasts.

My world was changing and Shandell, my mother, the TV, our bathroom mirror and I were all inadequate sources of information. I would've asked Shandell about some of the things I was dealing with, but I had no idea how to phrase it. I pretty much kept my questions to myself. Shandell and I talked some, but not that much. It's a good thing he and I didn't talk much more than we did about these things.

We would have led each other down a painfully uninformed and complicated road. We didn't know anything about sex or puberty, all we did was act like it. We worked so hard to fill in the gaps between what we did and didn't know that we actually started believing our own foolishness. For instance, it wasn't until years later that I found out that a girl can get pregnant the first time she has sex. I also learned that holding your penis at the base will not stop you from ejaculating, no matter how hard you squeeze. That was a lesson that came with its fair share of discomfort.

We flipped through the pages of life and puberty with the grace of drunken elephants. Each day we grappled with the scenarios written on its massive parchment. We rarely got the true meaning of the intended lesson until it was too late. We were teenagers being raised by parents who had no clue how to be parents, because they skipped being teenagers. This made them more of a hindrance than help.

Our parents didn't know how to give guidance or deal with our failures. Without someone to reinforce what we learned each day, our lessons were as permanent as a hopscotch game written on the sidewalk in chalk. The decisions we faced didn't match the information and the guidance available for our consumption. It took me a long time to realize that a bad choice wasn't the result of a bad person, but a person who, because of a lack of information or guidance, wasn't ready to make that decision. Until I figured this out I thought the world was just full of bad people.

In 1984 we were freshman at University City High School. Marvin Gaye would die, Run DMC was *Raising Hell* and everybody had either suede Pumas or shell toed Adidas with fat shoe strings in them. Brown kids could be found on street corners, on top of squares of linoleum wearing nylon sweat suits, Coca Cola shirts and spinning on any part of their body that would hold them. *Beat Street* was the King of the Beat and LEE Jeans with starched creases were the 'joint'. Shabbado locked up the girls and El had "All this Love" both confirmed that good hair and light skin were in. You couldn't be 'fresh' without a bomber and Michael's Moonwalk was one giant leap for street dancing.

Shandell was fourteen and I was fifteen. There were two things that were important in our lives, football and girls. We developed a propensity for both. I'm not sure if the girls were around because we played football or if we played to get girls. The game was a microcosm of the life that was to come.

Playing football, we met things that were bigger than us, situations in which we weren't allowed to think, we just had to react. We thought it could teach us all we needed to know to deal with some of the most important decisions of our lives. All of the people we met were through football. Our status in school was attached to our string on the field. We were freshmen, a lower life form than pond scum. No longer were we the two baddest things around. Entering into high school made us sexual algae, a frog was more likely to get a kiss. At the hands of the upperclassmen we suffered something we never suffered before, humiliation.

Each season started in the summer with a week of double sessions. This meant we'd start practicing at 8:00 a.m. until 12 noon, eat lunch, and then resume practice at 1:00 p.m. until five. Throughout the week we were at the mercy of our coaches and the upperclassmen. It was the coaches' job to whip us into shape and it was the job of the upperclassmen to whip us. Administering pain and humiliation were the upperclassmen's purpose. We were ordered around like slaves. They forced us to pick that up, drag this and by the time the coaches added in the rigors of practice, we were exhausted.

Shandell and I went through it all together. We were both running backs. He played the right and I played the left halfback and we were no joke. Neither Shandell nor I were small for our age. We weighed 165 and 160, respectively. Our size, coupled with our attitudes and rattle snake temperament, made us the best freshmen out there. Some people even said we were a threat to the senior starters. This didn't sit well with them. Our reputation for being bad asses preceded us and the upperclassmen were committed to humbling us.

On the first day of doubles all of the freshmen ate lunch together. We huddled in the locker room like squirrels with nervous conditions. We knew that random attacks on freshmen by packs of crazed upperclassmen were more than ritual, they were their duty. Our eyes peered over our hoagies that we gripped with both hands. Every sound caused all twenty of us to pop our heads up in unison. No sound was too faint to warrant the exact collective response. All of us used to be bad at our respective junior highs or middle schools, but now we all sat in a locker room scared, with our eyes bulging out of our heads. Once a proud bunch of young men, we cautiously gathered our nuts.

Initiation week was steeped in tradition. Pain was a fixture in its rituals. Our role as freshmen was to take the pain until the upperclassmen got tired of beating the hell out of us or until perpetuity, whichever came first. Everybody who'd ever played football at University City High School had abided by these rules.

As we ate lunch, our bodies winced, anticipating the blows that were inevitable. With every second that passed we regressed deeper into the corner of our locker room for safety. Nobody said a word throughout the entire lunch. The only sounds we made were our slow, deliberate unfolding and folding of hoagie wrappers. Stalked by seasoned predators, we awaited our doom.

"Hey!" our heads shot up. Eric, one of the herd of freshmen, swallowed an entire plastic packet of catsup that he'd been gingerly opening with his teeth. He didn't say a word, he just gulped. Our heads turned to see an ominous figure standing before us, his evil blackened the doorway. We were caged, trapped by our own quest for refuge. His presence filled the entrance preventing air from coming in. It was only a second between his first and next word, but in the time that elapsed I swear I heard somebody start crying.

"Captain's meeting! In the small gym! In one minute! Be there or else..." Then he left, unplugging the doorway. Air rushed in, filling the room, reminding us that we were still alive, but for how much longer?

The first words spoken following the Grim Reaper's visit were, "I ain't goin'," and yes, they were among the dumbest I'd ever heard. This bumbling idiot acted like he had a choice. This was not Burger King and he was not being asked if he wanted it his way. He wasn't being asked a damn thing and everyone reminded him of his total misunderstanding of the situation, "You goddamn fool! Have you lost your freakin' mind?!"

It was real. Destiny had entered our lives and taken us by the hand. She removed our backs from the metal lockers, lifted us from the wooden benches and brought us into the small gym. When we arrived she showed us that we were outnumbered and out-manned. Shandell looked at me and slowly nodded. I looked back at him and did the same. I knew he had my back and he knew I had his. Destiny had taken us to a strange place where the upperclassmen screamed and hollered things like 'Welcome ladies'. She'd brought all twenty of us, a quivering mass dripping with panic, standing silently, into this strange place. Destiny brought us this far and only she knew where we were headed.

The small gym was a three-ring circus of mayhem. Among the many techniques of administering pain was the "gauntlet." It was a cross between a Soul Train Line and a 'mosh pit'. This involved two lines of upperclassmen who faced each other. A space was left for someone to walk between the two rows of upperclassmen. As the victim made his way through the narrow alley, the people in the two lines, punched, pushed, spit on and kicked him. While they were setting up the gauntlet lines, the upperclassmen that were not involved accosted and then sequestered us throughout the gym. On one side of the gym they had guys on their knees with their noses to the gym floor ready to push a grape from sideline to sideline. On each of their backs there were upperclassmen riding them like horses screaming 'giddy up!' I could barely see what was going on over there. I stood at the gates of the gauntlet. All I knew was that the upperclassmen over there had a ten-pound medicine ball.

They told me since I was so 'big and bad' I had to go through the gauntlet first. My heart raced. I clinched my hands in and out, faster and faster. I waited as long as I could while they screamed obscenities at me, "C'mon you fuckin' fag... Oh, you ain't so tough now?....'dis bitch looks like he's gonna cry..." As I stood there absorbing their insults, somebody came behind and slammed me into the jaws of the gauntlet.

It was part of the ritual to walk through the chamber of pain. If the person going through tried to run, at the very least, they'd have to go through again.

When I took my first stumbling step into the punches firing like pistons I was stunned. With each step they came faster and faster, harder and harder. I trudged my way through, trying my best to stay on my feet, as the pain penetrated deeper. 'You can't fall damnit!' I kept telling myself. With each step the frequency and intensity of the blows increased as did the distance to the end of the gauntlet. I made it three quarters of the way through and then the density of hundreds of blows came in conflict with my path and my knees buckled. No one blow was taking my balance, it was all of them. I swayed from side to side like tall grass in the wind. Things seemed to be going in slow motion. My vision became blurry, my hands dropped to my side and I fell to my knees. When my knees hit the floor, I jolted. Instantly, I was hit flush on the chin. My head shot back. Limp, I began falling. The floor sped towards me. Its smooth cold surface collided with my right shoulder.

Immediately more than fifteen upperclassmen collapsed the lines and like starved wolves with a fresh kill, frantically swung and kicked me. It was a feeding frenzy as they tore at my flesh. They were yelling 'Get the fuck up big boy, you ain't so tough now bitch!' I was still conscious, although not entirely.

In the distance I heard Shandell. "Get the fuck up off of my boy!" The place erupted, wildfires had been set all over. Freshmen scattered everywhere. Everyone was going somewhere, but no one was headed anywhere. Most of the freshmen were running for the exits, leaving me to satiate the starving beasts. I could only hear them as they ran screaming, trying to escape where they were, by going places they'd never been.

From underneath the hill of bodies I could almost see Shandell. He was trying to break free from five guys who'd tackled him to the floor. I couldn't move or defend myself from the upperclassmen's oncoming fists seeking to maim, guided by tradition. Their feet and fists slammed into my skin and it answered with welts.

There were two major piles, mine and Shandell's. Upperclassmen not already involved in the piles were either running to get on top of one or trying to capture the escaping freshmen.

Shandell was struggling to get free as I lay there, a reluctant participant and interested spectator. He had one guy by the throat with his right hand and he was doing his best to throw a punch with his left. I could see the pile shifting as the upperclassmen tried relentlessly to break the wild colt. Each of them had lassoed one of his limbs. This swaying screaming mass shifted back and forth until, BOOM! Shandell freed his left arm and connected with a lineman's eye. The Rush had been the anchor for the pile. So when the fat bastard rolled off and curled into the fetal position, the pile shifted and Shandell was almost free.

Upperclassmen started breaking off my pile to restrain the run-a-way stallion, the Freshman. It was a melee. The mission was bigger than stopping Shandell from getting to me. If he broke free it would crush the foundation of this whole process.

Upperclassmen from my pile were too late. Shandell had broken free and he smelled blood. They were still coming from all directions to corral him. The pile on top of me had thinned, because more water was needed to put out the fire in Shandell's eyes. As they got off me, I started to feel a cross breeze, the result of doors at both ends of the gym being open, on my sweat glazed skin, but I still couldn't get to my feet. Once I recognized that no one was left on me, I struggled to steady myself onto all fours.

Shandell was tossing people on his way to me. In his path lay the injured pride of three upperclassmen. Just as he got to me, he was tackled from behind. He was stunned at first by the fall, but then he started fighting again to get back up. This time his fight was fruitless. Within a few seconds he was blanketed by the pack of wolves with something to prove. It was clear that there is nothing more dangerous than someone with something to prove, because they'll go to any length to prove it. The upperclassmen couldn't bear dealing with the implications of having lost control of the initiation to a freshman. This time they piled on top of Shandell with everything they had.

He fought and fought but he was pinned. They were screaming, "You think you're so goddamn bad?!" This huge junior named Scott loomed over Shandell with his legs straddling Shandell's head. Scott held the ten-pound medicine ball in between his hands and raised it above his head. Then, laughing nefariously, he yelled to Shandell, Let's see you get up now!" Then he dropped the leather ball on Shandell's head. CRACK!

When the ball hit Shandell's head it sounded like a two-ton light bulb had exploded. Shandell's eyes closed slowly and then his body went limp. His hands stopped swinging. His body was still. The ball slowly rolled a few inches and then stopped, almost as if to look back and survey the damage.

All eyes turned to Scott; faces were filled with disbelief. Nobody wanted it to go this far, but it did. The sound Shandell's head made as it hit the floor went through me like a lightening bolt. I shot to my feet, and in one motion, clocked Scott harder than I'd ever hit anyone in my entire life. When I hit him I felt the sensation of a grotesque intercourse as each of my knuckles had their way with his cheek. I hit that greasy bitch with more power than the force of gravity, because it was my punch, not the pull of the earth that dictated the direction he fell. When he hit the floor, he bounced and shook. He was out cold.

I started tossing those idiots who were still on top of my boy. As I got near the bottom, the ones still left on him got up before I could get to them. I was in an insane fit of violent wrath. There lay my friend. I looked at him for a second. As a huge knot rose from the back of his head and even bigger one filled my throat. I began to cry as I yelled, "GET THE DAMN DOCTOR!" Shandell lay there a gallant, fallen hero in a war that wasn't even worth fighting. He had become a casualty of circumstance and a victim of tradition. I started to cry. It was my friend, my heart that lay there on the floor, not a damn freshman!

The doctor arrived and Shandell was rushed in an ambulance to the University of Pennsylvania Medical Center. The word came back that he had a concussion and would be out for two to three weeks. He was going to be okay. I beat up Scott two or three other times that week. The second time I tried to kill him with a brick that was on the ground near where we were fighting, but the police came and I ran. The third time was just for fun. Scott was kicked off the team and fifteen seniors were suspended for a week, so was I, and so too was initiation week.

Shandell and I were heroes and from that point on they called us the "Two Horsemen", because of the way we bucked everyone off of us. In a place where there aren't enough heroes, even the children can lead.

Through growth we learn that some things no longer fit, while at the same time, growth allows us to reach things we never thought possible. Shandell and I looked and were beginning to feel like men. Change is rarely comfortable, but always inevitable. It was clear that our fort and all that it represented would forever exist in our memory as it disappeared from our lives. There is a point in time when, after having grown from a seed to a stem, a plant explodes, and blossoms into a flower. Our time was upon us or maybe we were upon it, but life was starting to look very different to and for us. Our vantage point had changed and with it, so did what we could see. For this, we could thank destiny. When working in concert with destiny, the flower is something of beauty, but with growth, even beauty changes.

Steve Perry

Split Decisions
Chapter 4

Our worlds clashed for a moment in time and no one was the clear victor. We were alone in the ring with trainers on the periphery barking overdue commands of guidance. When the final bell rang our worlds again parted. Our faces bore the pain and our hearts the cost of having received the day's lesson. Simultaneously we were friends and foes, learning together, competing for battle scars, winning nothing.

High school for Shandell and I revolved around football. Its fields of earthen fur were stages of dichotomy. Trampled by weekend warriors, the delicate blades of grass united to uplift two boys' dreams. These fertile lands were the surrogates from which recognition we received and the relationships we entered were birthed. Football is the sport of kings, played by boys, who were treated like royalty.

For what it was worth, we had a mediocre freshman season. Our underdeveloped legs curved in at the knees like young colts, standing for the first time. Sleek and full of life, Shandell and I were corralled by a wooden bench and the dust of limed sidelines. It was our eyes that took in the majesty of the striped grass. We were told that the reasons we never played were Anthony Chattanooga and Paul Fleming, senior running backs who the coach said had, 'paid their dues.' This translated into, 'here are two people who I like and, therefore, they will play even if they aren't the best on the team.' The coach's philosophy and the white lines of dust proved to be the impenetrable barriers, keeping us from getting too intimate with the playing field as freshmen. Without the peculiar ecstasy that comes from tasting the thrill of battle, we were hungry, no, starving. Running up and down the sidelines, we cut our teeth on plastic mouthpieces, chewed beyond recognition out of frustration.

We knew that we were the two best 'backs on the team, varsity or otherwise, and so did coach Norman Jimmerson. Sitting us down did nothing more than show the ignorance in Jimmerson's sense of duty to the two seniors. As a coach his decisions had always been suspect to those in the community who followed University City football, but we were seeing it first hand. It was obvious that he was more interested in keeping those two clowns happy than he was in winning games. At best he'd had a five hundred season, but that didn't seem to bother him. We'd heard that upperclassmen start on his team no matter what, but we thought we were different for two reasons. First, we knew we were better than everyone else and second, he said he shared our opinion. Early in the season he'd pulled Shandell and me aside and give us the 'you'll get your chance' speech, but that was crap and he knew it. The trouble was we didn't.

After we lost our fifth out of six games, and Anthony and Paul had combined for a dismal 30 yards, I was pissed. Throughout that game I paced up and down the sidelines. I just knew that Jimmerson was going to give us our shot that game. We were getting killed and when Paul fumbled on the opening possession and a Simon Gratz High School lineman took it back 20 yards for a touchdown, Jimmerson didn't even look our way. It was like he was consciously ignoring us. I wanted to kick the coach's ass. This was not just a want of, 'hey I'm so angry I could hit my coach', I straight wanted to choke him. I had it all planned. In the second quarter I told Shandell that when Jimmerson goes to his car after the game we should sneak up on him. I rambled on for the entire first half of the game and Shandell dutifully listened, but as the final horn sounded and we headed into the locker room for halftime, Shandell calmly told me to chill. He said, "I'll take care of Jimmerson." After that he didn't say another word. By the fourth quarter, we were down by two touchdowns and Jimmerson still didn't give us the nod. I couldn't remember the last time I was that mad.

We ended up losing that game by three touchdowns, because Paul fumbled for the second time and Gratz scored again. On our way back to the locker room Shandell broke his silence, "Yo Tarique, I ain't takin' this shit no more. We are way better than those two faggots. Just 'cause we freshmen, we can't get no play? That's straight up bullshit man!" I agreed with him. I told him that I thought that we should just hurt Jimmerson. Shandell again told me to chill and he didn't say another word. We got out of our pads and headed to the showers. After we showered Shandell said, "I'm goin' into that fool's office to tell him something." His plan was to enlighten Coach Jimmerson to the fact that leaving us on the bench was the worst coaching move in the history of coaching. Even being as mad as I was, I could tell that this plan had trouble written all over it. Shandell never said much to anyone but me, when he did, he didn't hold back. He said what he felt. This made people uneasy around him. His boyish face, broad shoulders and bad attitude made him somebody nobody wanted to mess with. They didn't know how to take him. His silence was intimidating to most people, including adults. It was also engaging. People wanted to get to know him. They'd always ask me what he was really like. I would tell them that they were stupid for asking me a dumb question and if they wanted to know, they should ask him. They usually didn't. But they were right to ask me, because we were so tight. There came a time when I could literally finish his sentences and he could finish mine. Being that tight meant that since Shandell said he was going into the coach's office, I was going too. It was a given. There was never a question as to what I was supposed to do if he had a beef.

When we got into Jimmerson's office there were still a few assistant coaches mulling around, trying to figure out the cause of our most recent shellacking. We didn't knock and we didn't wait to be invited in. I pushed the door open and Shandell walked in. Everything in the room stopped. Jimmerson was sitting behind his desk. All of the assistants looked at us as if they were trying to silently persuade us to leave before Jimmerson, whose job was on the line, saw us. We didn't budge.

"What in the hell do you want?!" Jimmerson exploded, his

words shaking the room.

Before he could close his mouth from the last word of his sentence, Shandell was up on him. I stood watch like the Fruit of Islam during a Farrakhan speech, "This mess don't make no Goddamn sense! Me and my boy Tarique are way better than those faggots you got running the ball now." You can imagine Jimmerson's reaction to being confronted by an arrogant fourteen and an equally arrogant fifteen year-old who together had never played a single down on anything but a street.

Jimmerson flipped. When Coach Jimmerson vaulted to his feet, threw his clipboard to the floor, and leaned over his desk, ending up nose to nose with him, Shandell's chiseled face didn't flinch. Their eyes were still for a second, as was the rest of the room. Jimmerson grunted through his clinched teeth, "What makes you think that you are so goddamn good boy?"

With his arms folded in front of him, probably trying to catch some of the overflow of his own arrogance before he spilled too much at once, Shandell calmly answered, "If you don't know by now, you mus' not have been at no practices." He punctuated his statement with a cool, extended, "...shoooot" and then he sucked his teeth.

Gripping his desk from beneath the middle drawer, as if he was getting ready to flip it onto Shandell's lap, Jimmerson bellowed, "You said it right goddamn it, PRACTICE! How many goddamn points did we get in this week's game from last week's practice?"

With his face as serious as a surgeon performing a triple bypass Shandell answered, "I might not know how many points we got from practice, but I damn sure know how many we didn't get in the game." The entire room, even people in the pictures on the wall, gasped in utter amazement. Even I thought, 'Damn bra' that's kinda' deep.'

It was clear that Shandell had done it. He'd made this man madder than he'd ever been in his life. If Coach Jimmerson's face was a monitor, it would've registered a systems overload. He was so mad he couldn't even yell anymore. The best Jimmerson could do was sit down, take a deep breath, and calmly say, "Get these two FRESHMEN out of my face." We were rushed out of the office by a platoon of assistant coaches who wanted a reason to run anyway.

I can't say that Shandell's speech got us any closer to the field that season. We sat the pine for the next three games. It did seem like Shandell made an impact though. Those next three games were played with juniors, Jeff Gallaher and Jay Robinson, instead of the two who had 'paid their dues'. We still lost all three games. Jimmerson did put us in during the last thirty five seconds of the last varsity game of the season. We were getting blown out 28 to 10, neither one of us ever touched the ball, it was a cruel joke.

Our sophomore year didn't go as bad, for us or the team. During the entire summer leading up to the 1985/1986 season Shandell and I worked out like madmen. While everybody else chilled and dressed like Miami Vice flunkies in pastels with no socks, we ran and lifted everyday. Infant hip hop screamed from its portable Sony cradles while we woke up at 6:00 a.m. to work out until noon. Janet was in "Control" and we were in the weight room. Club Nouveau offered up a shoulder to lean on, but we declined. We didn't see anybody. It was just Shandell and I all summer.

That summer brought us closer than we'd ever been. It's hard to spend every hour in a day with somebody you're already cool with and not get closer. When people saw us they said that we were starting to look alike. I have to admit, we were starting to favor one another, but this was probably because we were usually wearing each other's clothes. By the time we entered high school Shandell lived with us. He had even stopped calling my mother Mrs. Oakman and started calling her "ma". It only seemed right and she loved it. She told everyone she had two sons. When she went shopping for clothes, if she got me a blue sweatshirt, Shandell got a red one. There was as much of his clothes in my dresser as there was of mine in his. He had had some of my stuff for so long that he thought it was his. The only way I found things of mine that were lost in action was if I saw Shandell wearing it. "Yo, ain't that my shirt?" was usually how we greeted each other in the morning. That was more of joke than a legitimate claiming of property. It didn't make a difference whose shirt it was or whose shorts they were. What was his was mine and mine his.

At the end of the summer we came into camp looking like football machines. I'll never forget our first day back. We went into the locker room for our initial weigh in and mouths dropped. When we got weighed in we could only have on our underwear, so when our muscular bodies were unveiled, people bugged. "Damn! What did y'all eat 'dis summa?" Of course, not everybody greeted us with the same words of admiration. Some people wouldn't give us the satisfaction of knowing that they too were impressed by a summer's worth of working out. We didn't care what our detractors thought. It was up to them how they spent their summer. If they chose to spend their time breakin' on cardboard, that was on them. That stuff was corny to us and besides, neither one of us could dance. We had the grace of rhinos. We must've been in another line when God handed out rhythm. "Yeah, dey all big, but les' see what 'dey can do on the field." And to the field we went.

After our Monday morning weigh in and other preliminary stuff, it was time to take the field. By lunch on Tuesday, we were named the "unofficial" starting varsity running backs for the following season, thereby dethroning the heirs, Jay and Jeff.

We ran with such strength and grace that the nickname which had been given to us in jest during initiation week had come to replace our names. For the rest of the week all everybody said was, "the 'Two Horsemen' ain't no joke," and we loved it. We wrote our new name on everything, desks, bathrooms and all around our building. We even got a few shirts and, with those iron-on letters, we spelled out "The 2 Horsemen" on the front and back. When someone wanted to know where one or both of us were they'd say, "Yo, you seen the Horsemen?" We were the Two Horsemen. The label spoke to all that we'd worked for and all that we would be.

We worked hard all summer and nothing was given to us. Everybody else could've done the same, but they chose to do otherwise. We had no ill feelings towards those who sat back and did nothing, but we knew we were the best things happening on the field. This is a mindset essential to any athlete, especially a football player. It doesn't hurt to realize that you're the best thing to ever do what you do. Arrogance is not an option on the field. It must come standard with a great running back. This attitude doesn't make for the best people, but between those chalked lines it is the way of the world.

By the third game of the season we'd won more games than we'd won in the two years prior. We were undefeated for the first time in the school's history and the Two Horsemen were the reason why. The Horsemen were on course to break the combined yardage record for sophomores in a single season. I was averaging just over 125 yards a game and Shandell was just under 90.

As the touchdowns added up, so did the girls. Girls of all ages knew our names. "Ohh Sha Sha," Shandell loved to hear the girls call him that, "how you doin'?" It's amazing what a little recognition does to some people. It not only changed the way we were viewed, but it also changed how we viewed ourselves. We believed the hype more than anybody. Girls were telling us that they liked things about us that we didn't even know existed, "T, I love that beauty mark on your neck." We believed in what they were saying so deeply that, in time, we expected this of them.

Some times, no matter where we were, in school, at an after game party, or just hangin' out together in our neighborhood, there were girls who'd at least say, 'hi'. We loved it. Not everybody on the team shared in our happiness. That's probably because, in some cases, the girls who made sure they greeted us were girls who somebody on the team liked.

Who a girl was with or who liked her didn't mean a damn thing to us. Our motto was, "If he can't take care of you, I will." We truly didn't care how our teammates felt. They weren't our friends before we started doing well, so who cared if they didn't like us now? Either their girls came to us or we'd go to them, so what. They didn't have to listen. Shandell said, "If those chumps can't control them, then that's their problem, not ours."

Shandell was real aggressive both on the field and off. He always said, "You gotta show' em who's boss," no matter who or what we were talking about. He reminded me a lot of my father.

Not even a handshake could be gentle. With both of them, everything was about showing how much stronger they were than everyone else. I remember watching my father with some of his friends. They'd come over, slap him five and within seconds he'd have their arm twisted behind their back or he'd be on the floor wrestling with them.

Shandell, my father and I were all bigger than everybody around us. It wasn't my thing to be wrestling with dudes, but the two of them didn't care who they got physical with. They got a rush out of exerting their will over other people. Shandell would punch somebody in the arm and then dare them to say something for no reason. If they said something, at the very least he'd call them a punk and he'd say, "Stop crying," when they'd complain. He knew I didn't wrestle. He had no misconceptions that if I got started, there weren't going to be any jokes. When I got into it with somebody it was for real and for keeps. This is why he never laid a hand on me. However, everybody else seemed to be comfortable with the notion that Shandell would do what he felt he had to do to get what he wanted. Even when it seemed like nothing was out-of-bounds, no one dared speak up, they left him alone.

The Horsemen would go to parties and when Shandell walked in, it was like the music finally arrived. All of the attention helped him to come out of his shell. No more would he talk only to me. I remember times when he'd be in the middle of two girls, an island on a sea of booty. The girls would be saying 'Sha Sha this' and 'Sha Sha that'. It was something to see. He wasn't just the life of the party. He was the reason people came. No matter where we were, there'd be people laughing and carrying on. I had so much fun watching him. I'd sometimes see him entertaining two and three girls at a time. And if the girls didn't come to him he'd go to them. He'd do something like lie across their laps if they were sitting on the couch. When he got a little liquor in him though, look out. It tickled me to see his big uncoordinated drunk ass trying to dance. We never had to buy liquor, because somebody always took care of us. This meant there was never a lull in the "Sha Sha Show". He'd dance on tables, break tables or, when he was feeling real nice, he'd get up on a table and take his clothes off while the entire party cheered uncontrollably. I'd sit back and laugh hysterically at his always entertaining antics.

I took care of my business more covertly. I used to tell Shandell that we can get more girls if they all think they are the only one. He said, "T man, I don't give a damn who knows. They know what they are gettin' into when they want to get with Sha Sha and so I give 'em what they want."

There is nothing like the smell of sweat, foam, plastic and mildew filled our dimly lit locker room. The radio blared after-practice sounds of Erik B and Rakim. The rap duo's funk combined with the funk of thirty teenage boys to create vibrating lockers and an atmosphere reeking of exhaustion. Our locker room was a place filled with grass stains, girlie pictures and rampant testosterone.

At the end of practice we'd remove our hard outer shells piece by piece. Slowly we took off the plastic veneers exposing our soft discolored skin exposing where every pad spent the last two hours. Methodically we moved into the showers. The cold shower tiles under our feet were enough to make us stand three quarters erect. Then screaming bullets of hot water would shatter the layers of grime on our tired skin and pound us into relaxation. As dirt made its way down the single drain at the far end of the showers, away went our lethargic movements. With each new pellet of water came life. When full life was restored, a chorus of bullshit arose like the steam from the showers, sung by naked teenage boys about things they alleged they'd done with girls.

By mid-season the older guys on the team started to tease Shandell and me about being virgins. This was the only thing they had on us. All season they said things like, "The reason why y'all could run so good is 'cause you got 'blue balls' from humpin' all the damn time." They'd also say that the reason girls liked us was because, "They know if they git wit' a real man, they are gonna get sexed! ... Wit' y'all two babies they know that they ain't gonna have to give up no draws." I often thought that the upperclassmen might have been right. Maybe that was the reason the girls felt safe with us. Even Shandell had not yet forced a woman to have sex with him. Unwanted kisses and groping was the extent of his actions at that point.

Shandell and I swore we weren't virgins. We couldn't let the upperclassmen know that they might be right about why girls were giving us the attention. One time I told everybody that our girlfriends went to a different school and that was why no one had seen them. Derrick, a junior defensive end, responded to that with, "If you lie on your dick, it'll shrink." I believed him, which put me in a difficult situation. I didn't want a smaller dick and I didn't want them to know I was a virgin. From that point on I treaded delicately around the truth, I felt that my dick was depending on me.

Any time I said something, Shandell would confirm it and vice versa. One day, as we finished getting dressed and got ready to catch the bus home, I was 'treading delicately around the truth' about how many women we'd slept with and Jay Robinson, who hated us for taking his starting job, said, "The reason y'all know so much 'bout each others' sex lives is 'cause y'all is screwing each other." That one hurt. No one ever questioned our manhood to our faces without paying for it. Exaggerated laughter and, "Ooh that's cold," from an entire team lead by jealous upperclassmen bounced off the lockers, hitting us like daggers. To be questioned of our manhood was the greatest of pains. If we had nothing, we at least thought we were men. Others joined in on the barrage of insults, "Man, y'all always talkin' 'bout you be gettin' some, but you ain't got no proof." Cole Camp, a displaced running back who was forced to play defensive end, provided us with his little comment. His statement was followed by a chorus of 'YEAHS'. I knew if the girls in the school and around our block found this stuff out, we'd never get another call. The only looks the Horsemen would get would be to point out that we were THE two virgins.

I knew we weren't the only virgins on the team, but we were the ones being made fun of. Our teammates' laughter got louder and louder. My heart started to beat faster and faster. I felt blood moving through me, peeking as the laughter reached its zenith. "All right goddamn it!," I screamed, "You want proof I'll, no, we'll, give it to you!" I point to Shandell.

The laughter stopped for a second. Cole's voice, exhausted from laughing, ascended from the pause, "No he didn't say he'd give proof! How you gonna prove you got some draws?" I didn't know the answer and apparently neither did Shandell, who was looking at me as if to say 'what in the world did you get us into?' I had to answer Cole's question before the laughter..., it was too late, it started again. I had to quell the now obnoxious laughter inflating the locker room. I had to think of a way to prove we had had sex.

A few weeks before this incident Shandell and I saw *Sixteen Candles*. In it the two main characters were faced with the similar situation. They solved it by offering to return from their hunt in the bush with a trophy, the quarry's underwear. I told everybody we would bring to practice the girls' underwear as proof of a successful journey into the juvenile shrubbery. As soon as I said it I realized that my mouth had written a check my butt couldn't cash. 'Who in the hell is gonna give us a pair of their underwear?' I thought to myself. The laughter slowed with my statement, it never again fully stopped. But enough of them heard what I'd said to commit Shandell and me to doing it.

Cole said, "Aw right damn it, bring the girls' draws to practice in two days and don't even try to bring your mother's draws up in here because we all know what they look like!" Without saying a word, Shandell jumped up on the word 'mother' and by the time Cole got to 'like' Shandell was choking the life out of him. I grabbed Shandell, pulled him off of Cole and told him to chill. After I pried Shandell's hands from around his neck, while Cole, gasping for air, slumped over and held his throat. As he coughed and tried to catch his breath he said, "Somebody better control that crazy bastard!"

Shandell just looked at him with a sinister smile. Shandell was fiercely protective of ma'. No one, not even I, could say a bad word about her, and I didn't. He didn't joke, or play the dozens. Ma' was not a joke. I often felt that she meant more to him than me or his own life. If my mother asked Shandell to bring her a star, he'd come home with the constellation of Orion in a duffle bag. When she spoke he hung on her every word and when she came home late, it was he who stayed up until she got home. I'd always fall asleep first. There was nothing Shandell wouldn't do for ma', as there was nothing she wouldn't do for him. Cole really made a wrong turn with that crack. If I hadn't grabbed Shandell, things would have gotten very serious very fast.

I had Shandell in a bear hug with his arms pinned to his side. I whispered to him, "Don't worry about that idiot," as I started to drag him out of the locker room. He struggled a bit, but when he stopped focusing on killing Cole and recognized that it was me who was restraining him, he began to calm down. At the same time, I assured Cole and the rest of the team that we'd follow through and they'd get the precious underwear.

As I struggled to get Shandell out of the locker room he still hadn't said a word. Accept for a grin, his face was still, displaying no evidence that seconds before he was seriously going to choke Cole to death. Although Shandell's face was blank, his body struggled to be free. I'd maneuvered myself between Shandell and Cole. Shandell and I were chest to chest. We'd almost made it to the door leading out of the locker room when I heard Cole, who was trying to act like he wasn't scared, say in the background, "That boy better watch out, 'cause one day somebody is gonna take his ass out. Ain't nobody that damn bad that they can't be taken out." Shandell, still not having said a word, made one last leap for him. Cole crossed his arms in front of his face and braced himself, but I had Shandell locked up. I started to laugh when Cole, who was supposed to be all this and that, cowered in the corner like a little girl. When I started laughing Shandell finally calmed down. Without fail, if Shandell saw me laughing, no matter what we were doing, he'd start to laugh too. My bear hug turned into a hug and we started to laugh so hard that we had to hold onto each other to stop from falling. I was also laughing because, even though everybody saw Shandell jump on Cole, not one person moved or dared touch him to save that fool's life. I have no doubt that Cole should thank God that the Horsemen were never apart. If I hadn't been there, nobody would've been able to stop Shandell from killing Cole.

Now came the tough part. How exactly were we going to do this sex thing? There were a lot of girls who said they liked us but neither one of us had ever tried to have sex with any of them. We knew of the football groupies who apparently would do it with anybody on the team, but with that type of girl comes with a few risks. Disease was one, but more important was the embarrassment of them possibly saying no. If they said no, everybody in the entire city would know within seconds. We'd be ruined. Guys would laugh and girls would look at us like we stunk.

We decided to mess with these two girls, Selena and Gina, they were friends. We chose them for a few reasons. First, the Horsemen had dry humped them a few times. Second, they were close, so we could get them both in the same house at the same time. The third reason was that the Horsemen were operating on a negative budget, we couldn't pay for a motel, and although I was sixteen, I had no money for a car. All we had was my mother's apartment. The fourth reason was that my mother worked until 5:00 pm. This meant we had plenty of time. The final reason we picked Selena and Gina was because they hadn't been with a lot of guys. Everybody knows virgin wool is the best you can get. The Horsemen calculated our chances of actually getting some booty from these two. We knew it'd work. We talked to Selena and Gina on the phone individually about it. Shandell was on the other line when I talked to Gina and I was on the other line when he talked to Selena. They seemed to be down. We set it up.

The most difficult part of the whole ordeal was buying the rubbers. First we had to decide which store to go to. We couldn't go to one in our neighborhood because if somebody came in who knew us, it would be too embarrassing. We decided to go to the South Street to CVS where no one would know us. Neither one of us wanted to go in the store and so we flipped a coin. I lost. Before I went in Shandell said, "Yo man, you should buy some gum and stuff like that to go wit' the rubbers, so don't nobody notice that you in there jus' buyin' rubbers."

"What kind of rubbers do I git?" I asked.

"They come in different kinds?"

"OH MY GOD SHANDELL! You don't know they come in different kinds, damn man, we are through!"

"Naw, naw man, I was jus' kidding, get Trojans." He wasn't kidding, he didn't know there was more than one type of condom.

We both laughed anyway. I was laughing nervously and Shandell was laughing out of relief that he didn't have to go in and buy the damn things. What I meant when I asked him what kind to buy was lubricated or non. 'Trojan' was not the answer.

We pooled our money together and I went in. The whole time I could see Shandell through the doors directing me and laughing. I was looking for the aisle marked "rubbers" but I couldn't find it. This meant I had to go up and down every aisle, which kept me in the store much longer than I wanted to be. Apparently it was longer than the manager and security guard wanted me to be in there as well. They followed me up and down every aisle and when I'd turn around they'd turn away and act like they were arranging something on the shelf. Periodically they'd ask me "Can I help you?" They kept this up until I told them to, "Leave me the fuck alone!" They did. That's when the other security guard took over.

Finally I got to an aisle marked "Health and Beauty Aids". A wall of rubbers. There were some made of something called lamb, some had different tips and there were thousands of brands. I saw a big red package marked TROJAN. I thought the whole world could hear me exhale with relief. I picked them up like a proud puppy with a sock in its mouth and took them to the counter. There was no one in line. I must've had a sign on my forehead that said 'This is my first time buying rubbers so make a fool of me please!', because this is exactly what the clerk did. She fiddled with her drawer until there was a line bigger than the line at those check cashing places on the first and fifteenth. Then she yelled for a price check. It felt like the whole ordeal went on for days.

When I got outside I had to wait for Shandell to catch his breath. He'd been laughing so hard he couldn't talk. I, on the other hand, saw nothing funny. I knew we had to hurry home to meet Selena and Gina and we were running really late. I told Shandell to stop playing because we were supposed to have met them at our building at 2 p.m. and it was 1:45 and we hadn't even left the store. I knew it'd take us almost an hour to get home because we had to catch the bus and then we had to walk over five blocks to our building.

When we finally got to our building it was 2:45, the girls were already there and they were fuming. "We was just gettin' ready to leave!" they said in unison. There was no time to argue because, instead of having 3 or 4 hours to have sex with them, we only had 2. We had to be in and out, as quick as possible.

I nervously fiddled with the door to our building. I had so much on my mind. I was still reeling from my ordeal at CVS and I was getting nervous about my mother coming home. It was obvious that I was not the one to calm the girls down, get them to split up and then give up their draws in time to get them out before my mother got home. Shandell knew the situation and he could see I was falling apart as we walked up the stairs to the apartment. The elevator was broken. He could see that the more the girls yelled at us for being late the more nervous I became. As usual, he took over.

There was no time for small talk. Under normal circumstances the Horsemen would've left the room to make a plan and then come back in split the girls up and do our thing, which up to that point didn't require taking off anyone's clothes. But we couldn't leave Selena and Gina alone again. They'd made that abundantly clear. Shandell smoothly interjected as we walked up the stairs, "Come on ladies, you know the Horsemen ain't mean to be late, y'all know how we both feel about y'all..."

By the time we got to our apartment door they were in a trance. Without any prodding Selena walked off, headed in the direction of our room and Gina made herself at home on the couch.

There was no time for kissing and stuff. Back then my impression of foreplay was me taking off her clothes instead of making her do it herself. This time, Gina got no foreplay. I had one ear out listening to what was going on with Shandell and Selena and my other ear was listening for my mother as Gina and I undressed ourselves. Gina, was talking as we got undressed, I wasn't listening. I think she said something about this being her first time and loving me and some other stuff, I don't know. I was concentrating on how to get her to leave her underwear before she went home.

On the bus ride home from CVS Shandell and I had split the

rubbers. They came three to a package. Shandell got one, I got one and we decided to leave one in the bathroom just in case. When we were dividing them up, we noticed that they were "unlubricated". We'd soon find out how big of a mistake buying unlubricated condoms to have sex with two virgins was.

No foreplay. No attempt to make Gina feel comfortable and a rubber drier than an bicycle inner tube, made it almost impossible to have sex. Gina and I struggled for about ten minutes trying to get it in. Each time that we'd finally get it in, I'd lose my erection. Finally, after twenty minutes, I was in. In the distance I could hear Shandell cursing, "This dry ass rubber!" The Horsemen knew how important it was to use protection.

I remember thinking, 'I'm in!' I felt like I'd won the lotto. I couldn't believe it, I was actually having sex. Just as we got started she told me she was, "scared," and didn't, "want to get pregnant." I could tell by the look on her face that she wasn't only scared, she was in pain. She squirmed, winced, and moaned every time I moved. Making all of that noise was okay to me because it made me think that I was, shall we say, doing work. The more she squirmed, winced and moaned, the better I felt, so I tried harder to get it in.

"Trust me," I'd tell her. Then I'd lose my erection. Talking about babies can really ruin the mood. It's just as effective as the whole dead puppies visual. Every time I'd lose my erection we'd have to start over. By the time I was finally in and able to maintain my erection we'd been at it for over an hour.

Once I was up in there, what followed was to be the best minute or so of movement Selena ever had. "You're done! That's it!"

"This never happened to me before. I usually go for hours without stopping. I don't know what happened, it must be 'cause you feel so good that I just couldn't control myself. Besides, it's your fault that you can't keep me hard."

"Tarique, what are you saying?" she asked, looking painfully confused. "I told you I never did this. What am I supposed to do?" She started to cry.

"Shhh. Don't worry about it, I got another rubber in the

bathroom." I rushed into the bathroom, got the spare and went back in to try this sex thing again. I couldn't understand why I pulled up so lame the first time. Everybody on the team always talked about how they do it for hours. I wasn't going to be outdone, I'd show her.

In the distance I could hear Selena, they sounded like they were having fun, I couldn't let Shandell beat me. Gina and I again went through the same half hour struggle before we got started. This time it was a little better. We went for almost 3 minutes when, I heard the jingle of keys and then the door to our apartment flew open. My mother stood in the doorway.

My naked butt was sticking straight up in the air. I was facing the door, but my face had been buried in the arm of the couch. To make sure that I was seeing what I thought I was seeing, I peered over the couch's arm. Nobody moved. My mother calmly said, "I think that it is time for your friend to go." Gina slid from underneath me, stood up, pulled up her underwear, balled up her coat, gathered the rest of her stuff and got ready to go. I've never been so embarrassed. Then I thought, 'Oh my God, what about Shandell?!'

It was too late. My mother, still not having left the doorway, slowly turned her head towards the bedroom and a soundtrack of sex. "Who is that?," she asked.

"Oh Sha Sha! ... Oh, oh, OH!," hit the air and floated into my mother's ears.

"Shandell?," she said, a little bit louder than her normal speaking voice, "I think that it is time for your friend to go home too." The spring music stopped.

Shandell and Selena came out a few seconds later. Her skirt was tucked into her stockings, her hair looked like it had been teased so much that it had gotten an attitude. Shandell's shirt was unevenly buttoned. Both of the girls continually apologized as they bowed and backed out of the door like Asian concubines. After the girls got a short ways down the hall I heard them start running.

"Why don't you two boys go get washed up." Shandell hung his head in shame and started to walk out the door after Selena and Gina, but my mother said, "This is your home Shandell. Go in the bathroom and wash up." Shandell looked at her as if to ask her 'are you sure?'

"Yes, your bathroom, in this apartment." He was completely silent. He slowly began walking towards the bathroom and I followed.

While we were in their washing up, I asked Shandell how it was? He wouldn't talk to me. He almost looked like he wanted to cry. After we finished washing up, my mother called us into the living room and talked to us about sex, responsibility and babies for about and hour. Shandell looked at the floor the whole time. I'd never seen him like that. I didn't know how to take it. So I just let it go.

My mother sent us to bed after she felt she'd said enough. We went, neither one of us said a word. I didn't know why Shandell wasn't talking. I did know that I had a lot to say.

When we got into bed, I waited for a while before I said anything. Then, "So, how was Selena?," I asked.

After a very long silence I jumped on him and started tickling him. He pushed me off and started to smile. We laughed quietly and then he started telling me how he was tearing it up the whole time that they were in there, "Couldn't you hear her?" he asked.

"What happened wit y'all?" He responded.

"I was tearing it up too, couldn't you hear her?." I didn't know what else to say. I never experienced anything important without Shandell being one of the participants. I couldn't tell him that I was a minute-man. That was a strange feeling, lying to Shandell. I never felt I had to be anything more than what I was with him and now here I was lying about my sexual prowess.

I asked him, "How did you get that dry ass rubber in?"

"It was too hard to get it in with that thing on."

"What!"

"Yeah man, I don't need no rubber I got control."

"Can you control disease?" My mouth hung wide open.

"Man stop acting like a little girl."

After he said that I let it go. I couldn't believe he took that chance, I thought we felt the same way about this sort of thing.

"Yo man, what about ma?" I thought he was over that. He seemed scared. As if she was going to beat him or something. This was strange because he wasn't scared of anybody, not even his own mother. "I don't want her to think of me like this yo. I really love ma'. She always treats me real good."

"Now your actin' like a little girl. Chill man. You ain't got nothin' to worry 'bout, she's just gonna keep on talkin' to us all week about sex and stuff."

"But yo man, I don't want to dis' her home."

"Look man, the Horsemen can do anything we want, we are grown. Nobody can stop us. So we listen to what she's got to say and go on about our business."

"Aw-ite yo," he said, not really convinced, but interested in moving on.

By the time we got to school the next day every single person, including a substitute teacher knew what had happened with Gina and Selena. We were laughing stocks for a whole week. We never did get the girls underwear, but everybody knew what we'd done so we took the laughter and wore it proudly around our necks. Selena and Gina never did speak to us again, but we didn't care, there were too many others to take their places.

At the end of our sophomore year we were the big men on campus. We knew more people and had less friends. Shandell had become even more aggressive with women. His motto was, "They know they want it and I'm gonna give it to them." The girls didn't seem to care. Sure I saw him make a few cry and that wasn't my particular style of getting the honeys but if they were with him they must have wanted it.

I still enjoyed watching him entertain at the parties while I took whatever girl was down with it. We were both predators, but Shandell was more of a lion going out and capturing his prey, and I was like a Venus fly trap. I'd sit back and let my enticing aroma lure the unsuspecting prey into my jaws and then, gulp, they were gone. I especially liked to take in the wayward girls whose boyfriends didn't appreciate them. I hated to see a good girl wasted like that. So I'd bring them into my stables.

To have a lot of girls meant to have access to three or more at any given time. We had a lot of girls. We weren't the Fonz or anything. We couldn't snap our fingers and have girls running. That stuff is fake. We could, however, call two to three girls at anytime and arrange a rendezvous, where at the very least we'd see some naked body parts.

School was a joke. We went, played football, got girls and lived for the day. We were young in more ways than one. We were learning a lot and once I discovered the joy of naked girls, I found no more reason to fight. Now I had something else to do. Shandell still enjoyed a good brawl, so if I wasn't busy with what's-her-name I'd pull him out of battle. I started thinking that I'd rather be inside kissing with my lips than outside getting them busted.

The crowds weren't a big draw for me anymore either. At the after game parties, I'd go off, because there was more of a chance of getting the draws if I was alone with the girl than in some big crowd. The less people knew about what I was doing, the more I was allowed to do. Shandell still loved the crowds. He used to revel in all the attention. Everybody use to yell, "Go Sha Sha, Go Sha Sha, Go!" and he'd have the party rockin'.

By our junior year the Horsemen blew away all of the competition both on and off of the field. The only worthy opponents we had were each other. It was an uncomfortable competition, but all predators have to eat something, even if it is their own.

We both had excellent seasons, however Coach Jimmerson didn't forget the way Shandell conducted himself that day in his office. Shandell was blacklisted and no colleges wanted a kid who had a bad attitude, so he got close to no mail from schools. Whereas, everyday before practice the coach would call me into his office to finger through the countless letters from almost ten colleges who were actively pursuing me.

Shandell was upset about the blacklisting. One day, right before a big game against Strawberry Mansion, he told me that he was going to go into Jimmerson's office to tell him how he felt. "I don't care 'bout that nigga' no way. He can't coach and I'm gonna tell him 'bout himself." True to form, Shandell said he was going to go in there and did. I had to meet this girl Rebecca in the auditorium behind the stage. I wasn't able to go into the coach's office with him that day. I'm not sure how things went. When I asked, he told me that I should have been there and I would know.

So I left it at that. Rebecca had big breasts.

Shandell was still sexing girls without a rubber. "I told you I got control man, stop actin' like a girl," he'd tell me when I tried to set him straight.

"Yo Shandell man, what if you get some girl pregnant?"

"Look man don't worry 'bout me, I can take care of myself."

Near the end of our junior season he met this white girl, Sarah, who he really liked. Although Shandell was always around a lot of people, he always had one steady girl even if only for a week, that girl would be his girl. Sarah was a little different. He really liked her. Even when he was with the other girls, no matter who they were he'd never kiss them. "When you kiss somebody, you gots ta' look them dead in their face and ain't no hoe that I like that much."

When they got together, he stopped telling me the intimate details and I stopped asking. We always used to compare notes as to things we were able to get the girls to do to or for us. Once I asked him about how Sara looked naked, because I never saw a white girl naked in person, he said, "Yo man, chill that's my girl." I scrunched my forehead and tilted my head to the side. I didn't know what difference it made who she was.

In the meantime the season went on, Shandell's performance on the field was nowhere near what, I, along with everyone else, knew he could do. To make matters worse, there was a freshman named Kenny Eddie who was ripping up the junior varsity. Jimmerson was looking for an excuse to pull Shandell off the field and deflate his ego. The pressure was on, but Shandell pretended not to hear the rumbling in the background.

With two games left in the season we'd locked up a trip to the District Championship, something University City High School had never done. The last two games were academic. With the game nearly over and a win in the bag, Shandell's play was called. It was a sweep around my end. I always blocked for him as he always did for me. Since the game was basically over, I eased up and he got leveled.

When we got back to the huddle I couldn't stop laughing, "Yo Shandell man, you should've seen your face when that guy hit you," he didn't respond. His hands were on his knees and his head was down, so I stopped laughing long enough to squeeze out an apology, "My bus'."

He exploded on me like he had no idea who I was, "Your bus'!? If you do shit right the first time you ain't got to apologize!" I felt my heart beating in my throat. Nobody in the huddle said a word. Doug, our quarterback, interrupted the silence when he called the next play. We broke the huddle and Shandell limped back to the line of scrimmage. Shandell limped through the next three plays until, with two minutes left in the game Coach Jimmerson pulled him out and put the freshman in.

The season ended, we won the District and the Horsemen were elected captains for the 1987-88 season, our senior year.

After the season, there was an annual college fair that served as a place to meet girls from other schools held at the Philadelphia Civic Center. The Horsemen and that white girl hung out together when we went. Almost halfway through the fair I spotted this bad brown-skinned babe, so I left Shandell and his girl and went to introduce myself. Introductions for the Horsemen usually consisted of saying our name and that was when the girl would say, "Oh, your him?" This girl had no idea who I was.

Her name was Bria. She wasn't like anybody I'd ever met. She didn't like football and didn't care that I played. Both of which she had no problem telling me. She said that she thought that the sport was dumb. That day, all she wanted to know was which colleges I had seen. Truth is I hadn't seen any. I'd spent all day looking for girls who I felt were looking for me. When I told her that I hadn't seen any she said, "Well are you gonna?"

"Yeah, yeah... I mean, I was just waiting for some of the lines to go down."

She told me that she was going to collect information from 15 colleges. She showed me a list that she had typed up the night before. She and her dad researched the fair's participants and she was on a mission. When she whipped out the list, I couldn't help but laugh. She walked away.

"Wait, wait, wait a minute. I wasn't laughin' at you, I was laughin' 'cause I'm happy to see that someone as beautiful as you is also smart." She stopped, looked back and smiled.

"If you'd like some help locating prospective colleges, you may walk with me. Otherwise, I'll see you la.."

I interrupted, "That would be great. Thank you." We spent all day together. We went out to lunch, well if you call a Chinese food truck going out to lunch. But I paid. We sat on the steps of the Philadelphia Civic Center which is a block away from the University of Pennsylvania. As we ate she told me how she wanted to go to an Ivy League school. I was too embarrassed to ask her what "Ivy League" meant, but she was so smart and so sweet to listen to that I would have listened to her if she were talking about paving a driveway.

Bria had so many plans. "After I graduate from high school I will attend college, then, during my summers I hope to get a great internship." There was another word I had no clue about 'internship'. "Ya see, I want to get into a great grad school..." Grad school? Lost again, but still happy. "Then by the time I'm 25, I'd like to be contemplating marriage and a family." I knew what a marriage and a family were, and when she said them, they sounded good together. The way she lit up as she talked about the future made it seem like there was such a thing as 'the future'. It was as if she was convincing me that there was a Santa Claus. She made the future seem real and the type of place I should want to be. The way she smiled, the way she laughed and the things she said made me feel as if the sun had finally decided to awaken.

We spent the whole day together. I got information from Temple, Drexel, West Chester, Newman and LaSalle. Each time we went to a table Bria would ask questions about minority enrollment, drop out rates, financial aid, job placement and graduate school admissions. I watched her mouth. I hung on her words, got lost in her dimples and counted the stars in her eyes. I cheered her on as she stumped the colleges' representatives.

At about 3:00 pm it was time to load the buses. I didn't hesitate to ask her for her number. She said no.

She wished me luck on getting into school and reminded me to meet with my guidance counselor as soon as possible. I asked her could I give her my number. She said that that wouldn't be necessary. She then suggested that I go to my school's library to research the schools we'd found. Then she got on the bus and didn't look back.

The sun had set and the day had ended.

"So, T, who was that girl that me and Shandell saw you wit'?" I looked at the white girl.

"What?"

"You know, 'dat dark skinned girl with the good hair."

"Huh?" Why in the hell was she talking to me? I didn't even like her fat ass. She had one of those Salt-n-Pepa asymmetrical haircuts, big dooky gold earrings and more chains around her neck than Mr. T. I tolerated her dirty looking ass because she was Shandell's girl, but she should have known better than to talk to me.

"What's wrong wit' your boy Shandell? Why is he trippin'?" She talked as if she'd been dipped in charcoal and stripped of every ounce of English instruction she'd ever received.

"Tarique, why ain't you answerin' Sara?"

I looked at the two of them hugging and kissing all over each other, shook my head and said, "I'm tired. It's been a long day."

"Whatever, you ain't got to have a fucked up attitude though," she said as she squeezed Shandell even tighter and threw her legs over his. I looked at both of them and laughed. Neither had a college brochure between them. For the whole ride home and for days to come I spent all my time thinking about Bria.

A day with Bria. The thought, the words and the reality of it made me happy. When I was with her that day I couldn't think of anything or anyone, but her. For weeks afterwards I wondered if I'd ever see her again, then I remembered that the Temple representative said that they were having an event for students interested in engineering and she invited her to come. I was there.

That day I rushed out of indoor track practice caught the trolley and then got on a bus to Temple University. The problem was that I didn't remember the building that the event was supposed to be in. Temple is a big school in a bad neighborhood so I ran from one locked building to another trying to find something about engineering. I spent an hour running like a burglar up and down Market Street. Finally I found a security guard. Out of breath and patience I asked, "Where is the engineering thing?"

"Huh?"

"The engineering thing,.. The thing for engineers.. You know, that engineering thing."

"Slow down young man. What are you talking about?"

"Ma'am," I lost it, "I'm trying to find this girl, she's like this tall, brown skinned, brown eyes, long hair and dimples."

"Is she okay?"

"Ma'am, she's perfect. I ain't tryin' to rescue her, I want to go with her."

"Oh." She smiled, "That's sweet."

"Sweet or not, I gotta find her."

"Well let me see."

"See what?"

"If that young lady standing behind you listening to us is the one you're lookin' for." I turned around slowly, praying that what I'd see would be those eyes, that mouth.

"Hello Tarique."

"Bria?"

"So that's her I take it?" The guard questioned.

"Ah, yes ma'am. Yes ma'am it is." I stared at this beautiful, perfect girl.

"And you are?" A man's voice butted in. I turned and saw a man in his early 40's in a suit and tie, extending his hand."

"Ah, Tarique sir. Tarique Oakman, Jr. sir."

"Well Tarique Oakman Jr. sir, I'm Bria's father, Dr. Julani Ghana. It's a pleasure to meet you. What brings you out here tonight?"

"Ah, well, ah, college sir." I suppose it would have been more believable if I'd stopped looking at Bria for at least one second while I was talking to him.

He laughed. "Don't you play football at University City?"

Still shaking his hand and looking at Bria, "Ah, yes sir, yes sir I do."

"Well I'm glad to see that you've come for the pre-engineering college fair, but you've missed it. Why don't the two of you exchange numbers so that Bria can inform you of what you've missed."

"Ah yes, sir, I think that'd be very good sir."

"Let go of my hand son."

From the first time we spoke. I could tell that Bria believed in me. She told me that there was more to life than football. "Once you take that helmet off for good, you will never again be as important to these people who claim to care so much about you." She also told me that there is more to college than sports. She promised to walk me through the application process. She was the first person to tell me about something called a 'major'; and I wanted her to. Sure, she could have walked me through anything and I would have followed, but I really wanted the things she was talking about. I had been cornered into living for today and she, she with her smile, those bright brown eyes and her confidence in me, opened up my world and I wanted her in it.

I never had anyone besides my mother care about me because I was me. Over the next seven months she showed me how good love could feel. Bria said her feelings had nothing to do with my being able to run fast or win games. She really loved me for me, but she told me she was only going to work as hard as I did. One time I told her, "I have lots of female friends."

She said, "If I'm your girlfriend you 'had' lots of female friends." Bria used to say, "If you want to talk to a girl, then talk to me." Just as she told me straight up about what she expected of me, she also could put her feelings into words that touched my soul. One night we were on the phone, about to hang up and out of nowhere she said, "Tarique, nothing anyone in the world could ever give me would mean more than having you. Your heart, your time and your thoughts are more precious than any gift." I couldn't do or say anything. I just looked at the phone, waiting for it to turn into something bad. I knew I'd find out that I was dreaming, but I wasn't sleeping or she'd say, 'Just kidding', but she didn't. I didn't say a word for about 15 seconds, "Tarique," she instinctively assured me, "yes, I meant every word. Please, think of me tonight before you go to sleep. I have to go, my mom wants me to finish my homework.... I love you..." I was still staring at the phone, "Tarique?," her words gently woke me.

"Oh yeah, I'm sorry Bre....Yeah, I love you too... I will, I mean I will think about you, ...tonight, I will think about you tonight, yeah, yeah, I'll think about you..."

"Tarique, I've really got to go."

"Okay, umm okay, have a nice night."

"You too," she said as she laughed and the phone clicked. 'Have a nice night', what was I thinking?

It was April 1987, and prom time. I knew who I was going with and that was my one and only, Bria. We'd been together since the College Fair in October. Shandell told that white girl to ask her mother if they could go together. It seemed simple enough. Her mother and father were two of the Horsemen's biggest fans. They were at every game and most of our practices. They knew every statistic and were the first to run down on the field when we won the District Championship. Apparently that wasn't enough for them to forget that Shandell was Black.

The word came back that they said no because, and I will never forget these words for as long as I live, "What would we do with a prom picture of someone who looks like that?" It was as if they were saying that Shandell was some grotesque creature.

He was hurt and hurt bad, but he, as usual, didn't show any emotion. He had never felt the biting sting of overt racism and he therefore hadn't built a tolerance for its deep scarring affect. He'd spent his entire life submerged in blackness. He had Black friends, went to a public school that sang the Black National Anthem at assemblies and shopped at Chinese corner stores. He had all of the components of an urban black neighborhood. The foreign bite of this form of ignorance did not allow him to think through his pain, all he could do was respond. "So I ain't never really like that girl no way!" We both knew he was lying, but he had to do something to gather what was left of his shattered heart and trampled pride. I left it at that. I couldn't really talk to him the day he found out because I could only see Bria a few times a week and so when she was free I had to go. I was on my way to meet her when the white girl called. I knew he'd understand.

Shandell ended up taking a gold digger named Stacey Trent to the prom. She only wanted to be around him because she thought he was going to go pro. She was sickening.

That night at the prom I pulled Shandell aside and told him I'd decided to go to college. In the years prior, we had said that we weren't going to go to college. We thought that it cost too much and therefore it was for rich white kids. We had made plans to stay in the Bottoms and open a business. We had fully accepted that we were poor and black. The knowledge of who we were also gave us insight into who the people in our neighborhood were. We knew that the poor black people we grew up around cared about a few things and looking good was at the top of the list. We knew that they would map out a budget, not to buy a home, but to get that expensive jacket that they'd seen at Wannamakers. Even more important than their clothes was their hair. Both men and women would plan a weekend around a hair appointment. This is why we were going to open a hair products store. It was going to be named "The Horsemen's Hair Supply." We had even picked out the store colors and designed a logo. Shandell could draw real well therefore he took care of the graphics. But over the past few months Bria kept talking to me about college. What she said made a lot of sense. Eventually selling perms didn't seem as important as it used to. She told me she liked smart men and I wanted to be all the things she liked.

When Shandell realized what I'd said he looked at me for a second without saying a word. "Yo, what's up man, ain't you happy for me? Me, you and Bria could all go to the same college and..."

"I ain't goin' to no damn college! They don't want you there. The place that they want you to go ain't got no damn dorms, it got bars or tombstones?"

"Whachu mean man? I'm gonna go to college and be somebody," I said as I proudly pointed to my chest.

"You are a poor black bastard from the goddamn projects like me, who in the hell you gonna be besides him. No matter where you go or what 'chu do you are always gonna be A GODDAMN

NIGGER! Get that shit through your head," he punctuated that statement by poking his finger into my chest in the spot where I had just removed mine.

I smacked his hand away and said, "Fuck you man! Maybe that's what your gonna be but..."

"But what? That girl done messed your head up T."

"Don't go there Shandell." I wasn't going to let him talk about Bria.

"Whatever man," he looked at me with the same sinister grin I'd seen him give before and then he half laughed, "You do what you gotta do. I'm going to get some ass, see ya'." He put the hand I'd just smacked away up to his forehead and saluted, turned and walked away laughing.

That night he got Stacey pregnant. I tried to convince him to get rid of it, and her but he said, "I ain't like my father. I ain't no punk who knocks a woman up and leaves her. Ma' taught us both betta' and you know that. Besides, I know it's gonna be a boy and I'm gonna name him after me." It killed me that I simply couldn't get through to him. No matter what I said he wouldn't listen. I didn't know if it was going to be a boy or a girl all I knew was that Stacey was pregnant and about to give birth to No Future for any of them. Boy or girl that would be theirs and the child's destiny. Shandell wouldn't listen.

He and Stacey fought every single day. When Snooky found out about Stacey being pregnant she disowned Shandell. She said, "I am too young to be a grandmother. I didn't want no baby in the first place and I damn sure don't want another one."

My mother wasn't happy, but she supported his decision. She told him that she was proud of him for, as she said, "Taking care of business." He definitely was doing that. The summer before our senior year Shandell was working forty-five hours a week. While he was 'taking care of business' he started hanging out with some older guys. They were all former heroes on the football field who were looking for their dreams at the bottom of a forty of Budweiser. After a while my mother and I barely saw him. I knew where he was. He was with the older guys on the corner. He only came home to get clothes and slip my mother and me a few dollars when he got paid. Otherwise I never saw him. Between working out and chillin' with Bria I was pretty busy too. Shandell and I didn't get to work out together at all that summer.

Although I was busy I did miss doing all the things we used to do. I felt our endless summer of sleepovers, football and girls slowly cooling, but I understood. The haze of hot asphalt was being replaced with the clarity of fall. The Horsemen's Hair Supply had faded into time. Replacing it were a pregnancy and fatherhood along with a relationship and SATs. The leaves had begun to change colors and were being persuaded by the wind to hop aboard and ride it to the ground. The days would soon become shorter and the winter of our relationship would soon be upon us.

By the time football season rolled around Shandell was out of shape. Sure he'd been working, but the main reason was that he'd been drinking a lot. He wasn't ready for our senior season. His mind and his heart weren't in it. He missed practices and was eventually stripped of his title of captain by Coach Jimmerson. Shandell's boys on the corner were filling his head with bullshit. They were telling him he didn't need the team. They told him that he could go pro without going to college if he just lifted weights. I can hear them now, "Yo man, you could do like I did and try out for the Eagles." There were two problems with what they were saying. First, they never tried out for anyone. The only team they were ever on was the Bottoms All-Bullshit Team. Second, Shandell believed them.

By mid season Shandell's lack of preparation showed through and he was benched. Again he was replaced by Kenny, now a sophomore. That game Kenny and I set a Philadelphia High School record for combined yards gained in a single game; shattering the one set by Shandell and me. Shandell told me, "Yo man, I'm going to tell the coach about this sitting me on the bench shit." He went. Kenny and I had interviews with the *Philadelphia Inquirer*. Jimmerson wouldn't let Shandell in his office. He quit the team.

Now it was all about me. I was being billed as the biggest thing to come out of University City in years. I had more women around me than ever. They didn't care who I was with. They'd flirt with me, invite me to parties, help me with my schoolwork and even let me cheat off of their tests. I could feel their butt and they'd show me their breast, all without breaking up with Bria or making them my girl. They wanted to have fun and, I was a 'fun' guy.

Bria went to Chestnut Hill Academy. Her school was over a twenty-minute car ride from mine. The distance and my lack of control made me free to do anything. I don't know if I was too big for one girl, but that's what it felt like. Besides, how could I be sure she wasn't doing the same thing? Pam, this girl who used to like me, would always ask me, "What makes you think she ain't doing the same thing at her school?" I didn't have an answer.

The week of December 11, 1987 that lead up to the District Championship was the toughest week of my life. The game had nothing to do with the week's difficulty. After our last game Bria had come down on the field and told me to call her when I got home. That night when I called her she got right to the point. "Hey Bre."

"Have you been messing with anybody else?" She said as if she didn't hear a word I'd said.

"Whachu talkin' about?" She caught me off guard. I thought that the reason that she wanted me to call her was so we could arrange plans to meet. It was Saturday and that was usually the only day that she could get her parents' car to come to see me. They hated that she was coming to the Bottoms and did everything in their power to stop her. They wanted me to come out there. It wasn't that they didn't like me. Dr. Ghana would always tell me that I could call on him if I ever needed help getting into school. They were just afraid that she'd get hurt. I understood.

"Tarique I am not in the mood," she said in an exasperated tone.

"Bria I don't know what you're talkin' about." I didn't know who in particular she was talking about, but I knew I'd been cheating. Suddenly I got worried that she could tell I was hiding something. I tried to turn the tables and got indignant, "Why? You fuckin' somebody?!"

"Tarique," she said, unfazed by my explosion, "I don't have time for this. You know I'm not and I know I'm not, so are you?"

"I don't know shit! You could be doin' anything over wit' 'dem white boys at your school!" I was screaming into the phone.

"I just thought I'd ask you," she responded calmly. I exhaled. I thought I was off the hook, then she said, "I stopped by your school Friday to pick you up after practice. My father gave me the car, because he could tell that I wanted to see you more than once a week. As a matter of fact, it was his idea that I surprise you. When I drove up, you had some girl up against the wall. I couldn't tell what you were doing, but I noticed she was wearing your football jacket. The one I bought." By the time she finished talking she was crying uncontrollably. She gasped for air as she attempted to speak her last few words.

I was silent, then I said softly, "Bree, that wasn't me."

"Do you think I'm a goddamn idiot! Who in the hell was it then? I only asked you because I thought you would at least be man enough to tell me the truth." Her crying made it very difficult to understand what she was saying, but I felt every word and I could hear every tear.

"Bree, babe, I can explain," I pleaded.

She sniffled a few times and gathered herself, "You don't need to. Good-bye." She hung up. I stood there with the receiver in my hand. I looked at it, puzzled, as if she was coming back. The click of the phone answered my blank stare. The dial tone soon chimed in and then the obnoxious sound that the phone makes when it's been left off the hook too long rang in my ear. Numb, I slowly hung up. I put my hands over my face and cried as I'd never cried before. My chest heaved in and out. I couldn't believe it, she was gone and it was all my fault. I immediately dropped to my knees, 'God please..., please..., if you could jus',' then I realized that I was asking God to do something He'd never done, relieve me of my pain. I stopped, crawled onto my bed and cried well into Sunday morning. My mother tried to talk to me, but I snapped at her. She responded in the same way. She told me that I brought this on myself and that it was the same selfish attitude that allowed me to snap at her that enabled me to cheat.

With one game left in the season, Bria had found out about what I was doing. Outside of my mother, I never cared about a female's crying. That night I could hear my mother's tears running down Bria's face. These are the truest of all tears, because they do not come without the deepest of pains. The pain that brought these tears to the surface was betrayal and like my mother, Bria put together enough strength to walk away from the relationship.

I went to school that Monday glazed over. My face had been beaten and swollen by love. That was the way I stayed pretty much all week. Everybody around me thought I was preoccupied with the game coming up on Saturday. The game was the furthest thing from my mind. Words that came out of people's mouths were an annoying hum, to which I responded with a half smile and nod. I didn't want to hear what they had to say. I was sick of being congratulated on a great season.

As the sun disappeared into the horizon, nothing was the same. The distinct images that had started to become clear to me were transformed into silhouettes, standing shadows, bleeding into the coolness of night. Subtle shades of blue gently consumed my decadence and buried it in darkness. I stared into the steadily approaching night, hoping that it would not rob me of direction, but it defied my hopes, stole my dreams and left me with nightmares.

Steve Perry

The Exploding Vase
Chapter 5

...blown asunder by the vastness of the incident, never again to stand together

The Horsemen were now endlessly drifting apart. Shandell was worried about work and his baby on the way. I had a game in a few days, SAT's to take and I was dealing with an emptiness once filled with Bria's love. Shandell and I still occasionally talked, but not about much. We had become friendly, no longer friends. Our conversations were sterile. The only thing they had in common with the way we used to talk was the level of respect we maintained for each other's space. There were still those taboo topics we'd established during our first summer together. I still cared about him, but we had unofficially gone our separate ways. We now spoke out of a strange sense of duty.

I rarely knew where he was staying because he never stayed in one place for too long. Therefore, most of what we talked about had to do with where he was staying. The week before the District Championship he spent most of his time at Ottis' house. Ottis was one of the older guys who Shandell looked up to. People thought Ottis sold drugs, but he just worked a lot. He was a mechanic. On the side he bought cars at the auctions, fixed them up and then sold them. Between the time he fixed them and sold them, he would drive the cars, showing off his work. This meant he had a different car every few months. When Shandell moved in with Ottis he told me that Ottis was teaching him about cars. The two of them were going to open a garage in the Bottoms. He said they had a name, logo, colors and everything.

I told him I was happy for them.

Even from those conversations I could tell he was unhappy. Although we'd drifted apart, we still had a connection. Sometimes when he called the house my mother would answer the phone. They'd talk and laugh like they always did. The two of them would be on the phone for twenty minutes before I'd talk to him. I'd hear my mother ask him how he was doing. I could tell by her response that he'd say he was doing well. Everyone knew he was lying. He knew it, I knew it and my mother knew too. She has this way of saying "O.K." that lets you know that she's willing to accept what you're saying until you're ready to tell her the truth. Throughout their conversations I'd hear her say things like, "O.K. Shandell. Well you know you still got a place to stay when you get ready to come home." I think hearing that hurt him more than it helped.

When he and I got on the phone for those few minutes, I could tell that he didn't want ma' to see him this way. He was thick headed and he wouldn't accept that she wasn't judging him. I tried a few times to convince him to come home, but he'd made up his mind and I knew how he was. Once his mind was made up, the topic was closed. After the second time he told me no, I never asked him again. Maybe I should have, but I didn't.

When he wasn't paying attention, his words would come out slow and drained. He'd ask, "T, is ma' doin' all right?" I'd assure him that, as she'd told him seconds before, she was doing just fine. But his questions about her told more about him. He wasn't doin' all right. He wanted to know if she was all right with him and what he was doing. He worshiped her. He knew that she didn't want him to be living the life he was living. He had gotten a girl pregnant that he didn't even like and he felt a strong sense of obligation for his unborn child. He and I barely had two words to say to each other, and he was without the only woman he ever loved, my mother. True as all of that was, he still wasn't prepared to let me know he was hurting. Even if he was ready to tell me he couldn't. We weren't friends like that anymore.

Everyday of that week leading up to the District Championship seemed like a year. I couldn't imagine ever making it through all five.

Wednesday Shandell called from a pay phone. Ottis didn't have a phone. "Whas' up nigga'?"

"Chillin'," I said with just enough energy to get the word past my lips.

"Ma' told me what happened."

"Whatever," I angrily said. I was upset with her for spreading my business. The conversation was short. It was cold outside and he said he only had fifty cents. He told me ma' told him to talk to me. He didn't seem interested in what I had to say. His tone was flat and curt. We both knew that if it wasn't for my mother he wouldn't have called, so out of respect to her we said what we had to say.

I told him what I'd tell anybody I wasn't especially cool with. I said I was over Bria and was seeing other girls. Even though he and I weren't tight he still knew me too well to think I was telling the truth. He had a way, very similar to my mother's, of saying, "All right," which let me know that he knew I was lying, but wasn't going to call me on it. I appreciated it.

"If you over her, get you some more tail." I know that he knew better, but he was hurting his own hurt, he didn't have time to think about mine.

"Forget you man. I gotta' go. Peace." I hung up without waiting for him to say anything. Bria wasn't a 'piece of tail'. She loved ME. Not anything I could do for her. I missed her more than I ever missed anyone in my life.

I had spent too much time being "T" and too little time taking care of Tarique. T was who they created, Tarique was who I was. He was the one that Bria exposed me to. T was indestructible, Tarique had been destroyed. My heart was a shambles and there I was exerting all my energy into trying to act like it wasn't, instead of accepting that it was. Everybody wanted me everywhere, but nobody wanted me to be where I wanted to be.

For the first time in my life I felt absolute pain. What compounded the pain was that I didn't know what to do to get past it. I tried to avoid it, but it was inescapable. I needed to talk to Bria, but I'd driven her away. I wanted to talk to Shandell, but he didn't understand. I was alone. I needed someone to hold me and I wanted someone to tell me that everything was going to be fine, but there was no one.

All that week Kenny and I were in the paper concerning the game. One day photographers came into our classes, went to practice and hung out with us in the locker room. I could not have cared less. Beauty is redefined when seen through the eyes of sorrow. A tear's smooth curves can blur even the Mona Lisa. Heartbreak is an emotional trek that causes physical fatigue. My anguish saddled me with a new perspective through which I viewed the festivities leading up to the game. After all, it was just a game.

Everywhere I went I heard, 'Ready for the game?' No one wanted to know how Tarique was doing. 'How's your arm, shoulder, back?', or whatever other body part they could reduce me to. What I wouldn't have given for Bria's sweet voice asking me how I was doing. She would've really cared.

I looked at the phone day and night. Every time it rang I'd run to it and every time I picked it up I was disappointed. It was always the same lame girl wanting to 'get together'. I couldn't imagine messing with some stank girl. When I realized it wasn't Bria I'd hang up. No matter how rude I was, she never stopped calling. Sometimes she called back to apologize, essentially, for doing nothing, and I'd hang up again.

There were times when I'd sit and watch fifteen minutes tick off the clock without moving a muscle. My life had been turned upside-down. Bria had changed me and she wasn't there to enjoy what she'd done.

The game came and went. We blew them out. I had one of the best games of my career. We were champions again. So what.

There was, as usual, a party after the game. A cheerleader named Karen who had a really nice house, was hosting it. I wasn't going. After I'd gotten home Shandell called me and congratulated me. That meant a lot. Knowing that all was not lost between us made me the happiest I'd been the entire week. Shandell always did know what to say. Words can heal wounds and shatter lives. They can sing a child to sleep and scar an infant's growth. Dancing in a song or tucked in a book, words are the symbols of a people. Shandell's words gently reminded me of a time when we were close. Their fingers ran across a dormant place in my mind, sweeping away the dust and pulling down the cobwebs. Shandell was home and I met him at the door.

"Yo T man, you goin' to the party?"

"Naw man, that stuff is wack."

"Wha's up man? Don't tell me you still thinkin' 'bout that girl."

"Whatever. Jus' forget about her. So how are Stacey and the baby?"

"That bitch is still crazy, but she's got my boy in her, so I got to stay wit' her. Anyway, tha's one of the reasons I wanted to know if you was goin' to the party. I got somethin' real important I want to ask you and I got something I think you need, a present."

"Why can't you jus' tell me what it is you got to say now? Besides, you know you ain't got to give me no present! 'Specially since your broke ass ain't got no money that Stacey ain't got claim to."

"Ahh, you funny. It's too important to say over the phone and fuck you and Stacey. You and her can kiss my hairy black ass, 'cause neither one of y'all know how much money I got. Man, is you gonna be there?"

"Damn man, I told you...," and then I caught myself. I realized that if Shandell said that it was important, then it was important, "...okay, I'll be there."

"BET! I'll try to meet you at ma's, but don't wait, 'cause if I miss you, I'll meet you there. Me, Ottis, Dyke, Derrick, James, Doug, Dario and them are gonna go get messed up before we go to Karen's, so..., you probably should jus' go ahead and meet me there." These were the rest of the older guys he'd been hanging with. He paused, then he said, "We gonna rip that matha' up tonight!" It was done. I was going. I still didn't want to go, but it was for my boy, I thought to myself, 'I can take these people for a little while.' Besides maybe being out would help me stop thinking about Bria for a few hours.

I waited for Shandell at my house for about twenty minutes, but he didn't show. The Horsemen usually didn't go to the parties until late. We liked to make a grand entrance. I was at the height of my fame. I knew that everybody would be waiting to see me. I made them wait. I wasn't feeling very much love for my "fans" anyway. Especially after realizing what this whole thing was about.

I meant nothing to them and it was about time I treated them the same way. All of the happiness I was experiencing was because I had a true friend and I was in love. With both of them gone I could see what was left. The cheers that I had longed for were empty screams, noise with no purpose or meaning. For those empty screams I had run and jumped without ever noticing that they held my reins. My thirst for attention left my mouth wide open for them to put an iron muzzle on my face and strap a plastic saddle to my back. Every week I went to Frank's barber shop on 39th and Locust to make sure my mane was groomed for each contest. I wasn't a 'Horseman', I was the horse, Black Beauty, a show pony. I was no more than an entertainer, a court jester, on a pedestal for their entertainment and now it was my turn to get mine and go on with my life. I'd suffered countless sleepless nights because I was worried about this play or that. On the field I was "the man", the key for opposing defenses. The relentless punishment I suffered aged my body five years. So I was going to go to Karen's party to eat up all of that girl's food, drink all of her beer and do whatever the hell I wanted. If we would've lost the game, my phone wouldn't be ringing and everybody wouldn't be smiling at me like family members staring at a newborn through the maternity ward glass. They'd gotten what they wanted from me and now it was my turn.

I was fed up. I'd allowed their empty compliments to expel one the most important people in my life. I hated myself for what I'd done to Bria, but I was too proud to call and apologize and I knew that even if I did she was not going to take me back. The only thing she'd done wrong was to trust me. I hated myself and everyone else who I felt I could blame for my pain.

When I got to the party somebody said, 'T's here!' People called me T when they wanted to act familiar. They'd heard Shandell say it, so they thought it was cool. With that announcement two girls made their way over to me. Mandingo was in the house. The sexual myth had arrived, six feet, two inches, two hundred and twenty pounds of black man. They were looking at me, but what they saw was in their head. I knew what these two were up to, I have to admit, it still felt good. I was addicted to them like crack. I was so strung out. I knew messing with these girls had crushed Bria and destroyed my life, but I still wanted to taste it.

Karen's place was packed. There were wall-to-wall people. It was December and it felt like summer in there. It was so hot that the walls were sweating. Karen's parents had put a lot of work into that house. The kitchen was to the right as you walked in, then the hallway opened up into this huge living room with sliding glass doors. There were crossing wooden spoons over her dining room table and in the living room there were two big pictures, one of Dr. King and the other of a Black Jesus. The living room was swaying back and forth. The music was booming when I got in there. When I stood still, I felt the floor rocking.

I took my normal perch, far enough back from the action to feel it but not be in the middle of it. Then I sat down and waited to see what was gonna happen. I was on the stairs facing the front door. I wanted to be sure I'd see Shandell when he got there, while at the same time I overlooked the whole party. I wasn't gonna get caught in the middle of all of that. Almost every party ended in some kind of brawl. A party wasn't a party without a fight. If nobody fought, people wouldn't know when to leave. They'd all just stay the night if the police didn't come and drag somebody's dumb ass away.

As soon as I sat down, people started bringing me drinks. I couldn't close my hands without somebody putting something in them. Each drink came with free advice on everything from my career to sex, 'Yo man, you should jus' go to 'da pros, bump college', 'You should hit that girl wit' the red skirt. She ain't neva gave it up to nobody, but you could git wit' it'. Midway through the night I was feeling pretty nice. No, I was totally drunk. I couldn't hear a word they were saying. I had a good buzz on and that was all I needed. It was time to get some honies.

In every corner there was something different going on. Enough people were smoking weed to create a thin gray cloud that danced along the top of the crowd. If I would have moved up a step the smoke would've engulfed me. Most of the people were trying to get in somebody else's pants. It was funny watching some of the freshmen. They probably had to beg their mothers to get out. I laughed out loud as they told girls how the coach told them that next year they're going to be the man. All night the same two girls took turns coming up to me. After a while I realized I didn't have it in me. My instinct was telling me to at least try to do something, but my heart wouldn't allow it. It was absolutely clear that they were nothing to me and I knew that I couldn't fake it. If I did anything, it would've been for somebody else and those people had gotten all they were going to get from me.

That night the only thing they were going to get from me was my ass to kiss. When those two girls stood in front of me telling me how cute this was and how fine that was, I'd tell them to move out of the way so I could see the door. I'd come there to see Shandell and after I talked to him I was out.

Finally he came. There was no announcement, but I saw him and I waved him over to me. I told the girls who were standing there, "I got business to take care, so if you don't mind," and then I motioned my hand to shoo them away. They left. Shandell ran up and hugged me, "My nigga, what's up!" He was more drunk than I was.

"Nothin' man, I'm jus' coolin' it. So what's up?" I asked.

"Damn man, wha's the hurry? I ain't seen your ugly ass in like a week. Can't I say what's up to my boy firs'?," Then he sat on my lap and wrapped his arms around me. When Shandell got drunk he either wanted to fight or have sex, sometimes both. But before he did either he had to hug on everybody. Alcohol messed him up. He would say or do anything. That's why he was so funny when he got drunk. Nobody knew what he was going to do. He always told people he loved them, no matter who they were. I don't know why he did it, but he did. He assured me that, "I'm gonna' get some booty tonight! Can't nobody say no to Sha Sha," punctuated with a drunken laugh, "ha ha ha." Nobody expected him to be faithful to Stacey. He made it clear to her and anybody who would listen that all he had done was have sex with her. He'd tell people he couldn't stand her. Now that she was having his baby he still didn't like her. It was no surprise that he'd set out to get some tail no matter what.

"Aw ite, this is what I got to tell you," he leaned into me as if he had a huge secret. "You know how much I love you right?"

"Yeah Shandell, I know...," it was my turn to be loved.

"Well, when Stacey has my baby I want you to be his Godfather."

"That's cool. What do I gotta do?"

"I don't know nigga! Jus' do whatever," he shrugged his shoulders and said. "I ain't never been nobody's daddy so how am I supposed to know?" Then he started laughing. I couldn't help but join in. "Oh wait!" he yelled, as loud as he could, even though his mouth was almost in my ear, "I told you I got somethin' I think you need, right?"

"Yes Shandell," I said patiently as I plugged my ear with my index finger to save it from any further damage.

"Well I went and got it, tha's what took me so long, wait." He fumbled through his pockets as he swayed back and forth, "Oops, it's outside." He jumped out of my lap and ran outside with a forty in one hand and the wall with the other. I watched his crazy ass stumble through the crowd, down the hall and out the front door. I felt my face smiling again. I noticed that for the first time in a week I was happy.

The next thing I knew I was laughing out loud, shaking my head and saying, "That nigga is silly." He was such a clown.

"What 'chu laughin' at Mr. Football?" this girl named Shari asked. She wasn't one of the two who'd been hounding me all night. I'd messed with her a few times over the years, but it'd been a while since the last time we had sex. She jumped up on my lap, straddled me and then she locked her arms and legs around me. "You are givin' me some tonight Mr. Football," she proclaimed as she started to grind me. She had on a tight mini skirt that showed all of her maturity. It showed even more when she jumped on me. As she sat on my lap her skirt had raised up around her waist, it looked like a belt by the time she got situated. Everybody behind her could see everything.

Before I could say a word, she slammed her tongue down my throat and then simultaneously I heard Shandell say, "Tada!" and from behind him stepped Bria, "Oopps, you look a little busy. We'll be right back!" He turned around and tried to shield Bria from seeing Shari with her tongue down my throat and her half naked ass humping my thighs. Shandell grabbed Bria and started to rush her back outside. It was too late.

"Get off me Shandell! I'm not a damn baby!" Bria turned her back to me, as if I wasn't there, faced Shandell and said, "I thought you said he missed me, he seems to be doing all right with this little slut." I was stunned. Shari hugged me even tighter and looked back at Bria and smiled. I couldn't say a word. It all happened so fast. No more than two seconds passed from Shari's kiss to when Bria's came in. Then Bria turned, looked me straight in the eyes and said, "Here is your goddamn present! Congratulations." She threw a gold bracelet at me. It hit Shari in the back, fell on the floor, then she took off into the dense crowd. The bracelet said 'I love you and miss you'.

"Oooops," Shandell cupped his hands over his mouth. "That was my surprise. I figured you wanted to see her..." Then, realizing that she wasn't coming back, Shandell told me to, "Hold up a minute. I'll go get her and explain what jus' happened before she goes home."

"Forget her man, I don't give a damn what she does. I ain't got time for her silly shit. She can do whatever the hell she wants. All she ever wanted was some dick. Now she can go and fuck some other nigga' if she wants. I ain't got time to be playing games, I'm TARIQUE."

"Naw T man, you don't mean 'dat," I looked away. "C'mon man, just chill for a second. Damn, why you so hyped?"

"Fuck her."

"Chill man, you don't mean that."

"I'm serious man, FUCK HER!"

"T...," I put my hand up to interrupt him with my palms facing him.

"Aw 'ite man, are you sure?"

I smiled and said deliberately, "Hell yeah."

"Naw, for real though, you really don't care?" I pointed to Shari, who was still sitting on my lap, laughed and nodded my head, as if to tell him that I had mine for the night. Shandell put his index finger and thumb together and made a circle, then he put his fingers up to his eye and said, "OOOOO KEE DOE KEE." After that he skipped off after her.

When Shandell left, Shari kissed me on the ear and whispered, "So where do you wanna do it?"

"Get the hell off me bitch!" I pushed her as hard as I could. She fell on her back and then her head slammed against the floor. She lay there for a second and started to cry. After a few seconds she stumbled to her feet. Holding the back of her head. "You ain't that good 'Minute Man'," she said with tears in her eyes, and walked off slumped over sobbing. I looked at her and laughed. I didn't mean to hurt her, but I wasn't going to apologize.

I grabbed my head and put my elbows on my knees in disgust. What in the world had I done? I kept looking down at the bracelet, it was still on the floor where Bria threw it. I was speechless. Bria was too proud to take my stupid ass back. She had her stuff together, she was headed to the University of Pennsylvania to study engineering on a full academic scholarship. We had had it all planned. I was supposed to play at Temple and she'd be at Penn. She promised me that if and only if I tried she'd help me with my studies, "I am not doing anyone's work and I will not marry some dumb jock." When she said that I just smiled. I didn't want to be a dumb jock I wanted to be all that she was to me. I wanted to be her world. I had no clue how to tell her that, but it was no less true.

She held up her part of the bargain. She was in at Penn. All I needed was a 700 on the SAT's and I would be in at Temple. She even helped me study for them. We were supposed to spend the rest of our lives together. If only I could tell her how I felt about her.

Just as I finished that thought, I looked up. The crowd was

parting for some girl who was stumbling through. I couldn't make out who she was, but she looked a mess. She was coming towards me faster than I could register her features. Then she fell at my feet. It was Bria.

The music stopped. She was crying uncontrollably, "I...I, He, He..., I told him no, but... but he wouldn't stop," was all she could say. Her clothes were torn and she was bleeding from a cut over her mouth and right eye. And an all too familiar red tear ran down her cheek. Her petite delicate frame was twisted with pain and shame. She tried to hold her blouse together, but there were no buttons left on it, it was shredded. "I'm sorry Tarique, I tried to stop him." I looked down at the girl at my feet. I couldn't move at first. Even as Bria's posture called out for comforting I was paralyzed with disbelief. All I could do was look down at her. At that moment Bria had become my mother. I remembered how I had sworn that when my father had beaten my mother out of her home, family and marriage, that that was the last time I would ever let a man harm a woman I loved. I had no choice as to what I had to do now. I had to follow through on my promise.

A few seconds past. I still hadn't moved. My eyes were fixed on Bria as she sobbed and fumbled to cover herself. Two feet entered the frame of the floor upon which Bria lie, one on each side of her. They shocked me into movement. I panned up from Bria. I saw a familiar set of legs buttressing a torso I'd seen. I couldn't recognize the face. His teeth protruded from a familiar, yet unfamiliar, sinister grin. His eyes were bloodshot. He was out of breath and panting. Blood dripped from his mouth. His handsome face stared back at me cloaked in pure evil. He stood over her with his clothes torn and blood escaping from three scratches on his cheek. When our eyes met, I squinted my left eye as if to ask 'how could you?'

He looked at me, shrugged his shoulders, and answered my eyes with a laugh, "What?" His voice chimed in my ears. It was Shandell.

Without a word I jumped over Bria and in one fluid motion hit him with everything I had. He fell and I was on top of him. Sun from a project playground again scorched our skin. Its rays of fire burned away what was left of a once magnificent friendship and left the hard shell of combat. He was my enemy.

Fists flew with the malice. We rolled back and forth struggling for position, swinging as hard as we could. The shag carpet erased patches of skin. My sweat forced his drunken hands to lose their grip. I broke free. I saw a broken bottle. Its jagged edges glistened in the moonlight, invited into the room by the sliding glass doors' translucence. As I crawled for it, he kicked me in the neck and I fell limp. I couldn't get up. The whole party grabbed him.

"Get up pretty boy! You never could beat me. You're soft, just like you always was!" I still couldn't move. I lay there on my back. My fingers and toes started to tingle. Kenny came behind me, slid his hands under my armpits and lifted me to my feet. I started to feel my hands and feet again. Within a few seconds, I was standing on my own.

I looked at him as I tried to regain my composure. We were still separated by the whole party. I had regained my composure and knew I wanted to hurt him. Shaking out the cobwebs I said, "You're no fuckin' good, jus' like your goddamn father!"

One of the older guys said, "Fuck that motha' fucka' Sha Sha, He ain't shit and he ain't neva' been shit!"

Shandell laughed and said, "You right," in response to that statement. Then he turned to me and said, "You talk about my father, ma' told me how you didn't do nothin' when your father beat the shit outta' her. Tha's why I thought it was okay to beat tha' shit out of your little whore and then fuck her." His words rang out like thunder detonating in the heavens, then cracking to the earth, where they exploded into an inferno. Their destructive force crushed the remnants of our relationship, exposing the taboo.

Nothing can stop the course of destiny, not even love. It is the most powerful force in the universe. No one or no thing could stop us. The hands of those who'd separated us were melted by the white hot river of molten lava raging through our veins. We broke free. There was no time or need for thought. The end was near and the moist cold stench of rigormortis was in the air. We shot towards each other. He swung first, but the venom of the serpent's ale still had control over his body. The force of his blow spun him around three hundred and sixty degrees. Just as he finished his turn, I got there. I lowered my shoulder into his chest, wrapped my arms around him and drove him through the huge smooth sliding glass doors. His back ripped open the window's tranquility and it let out a piercing scream. We were airborne. As we passed through the glass door we left our aggression behind. There was no conflict as we rode the night air to our destination. Together we glided in gentle silence. When we landed he let out an 'Uh.' We came to a complete stop.

There we lay, my right cheek on his chest, my arms still embracing him. I looked up at him full of questions. I felt like we were where we were supposed to be, but it didn't feel right. Neither one of us could move. His arms were outstretched on the wooden deck. His head hung lifelessly as blood stained and made soft the wood beneath us. In the background, what was left of the enormous window, continued to fall, making it impossible for anyone to follow our path of destruction.

He and I were alone. Our blood once again ran in unison. The blood that ran from his cheek, called to the surface by Bria's frantic hands, had dried. The blood that poured was ours. We were alone and cut off from the rest of the world, but we were not together.

He very slowly looked down at me, barely opening his eyes, "Yo man, My bus'," creaked out of his lips. His throat had been cut with precision by the giant window. And then he halfway smiled and very slowly said, "Who... is... gonna clean up.. all this glass...?" He then closed his eyes completely, wringing out a tear that ran down his cheek. It surfed the swollen waves of his face. Its smooth curves effortlessly met each interpretation of his formerly chiseled cheek. Then it leaped from his face. Gravity brought it home to an awaiting ruby pool. It playfully splashed, rippled and then blended in with the flowing tributaries of our blood.

Satin, Brass and Mahogany
Chapter 6

Sirens screamed through the streets announcing the arrival of a cadre of blue suits. The paramedics plowed their way through the still dense crowd, carefully stepped through the dangling glass and frantically began working on Shandell and me. They peeled our lifeless bodies apart and desperately looked for the origins of the tremendous flow of blood. After they separated us, I watched them work on Shandell. The people working on me fought to keep me conscious and when I was conscious, to keep me still. Instinctively I tried to move, but when I moved the glass in my skin cut deeper, creating a convulsion-like response.

The paramedics worked on my face and back. They were more concerned with my face. Endlessly flowing blood forced my eyes shut. Immediately after they realized that I had deep lacerations slightly above my eyelids continuing into my eyebrows, my eyes were bandaged. The last thing I remember about being at Karen's was the sounds. Each time I faded back into consciousness I'd hear women crying, the Emergency Technicians hollering back and forth to one another, the police trying to keep everybody back and myself, yelling for anybody who'd listen to do anything they could to stop the pain.

Pain awakened me in my bed at Hannaman Hospital on Sunday morning. My eyes were still bandaged, I had no way of seeing what was happening around me, but pain stepped forward to be my guide. First it walked me down a deserted side street and left me there. Then when I moved to seek the comfort of a familiar position, it returned to torment me, penetrating me on the wings of screaming bats. Menacingly perched atop the bats like a hoodlum roaring through the streets on a

131

Harley, it'd command me to stay where it left me. After pain's first assaults, I began to brace myself while a lump formed in my throat. As soon as I felt confident enough to again attempt to leave the terrible position I was in, pain rose out of nowhere, dripping with lifetimes of tears to meet me. Standing in front of me, pain opened its eyes like two moons rising at dusk. Then it slowly closed them, like the sun at dawn, daring me to try to move again.

Lying in pain's shadow I could tell it knew that it was going to have control of me for a while. I watched it take its time as it prepared to overcome me. Arrogantly it advanced, slowly and deliberately, covering ten feet with each stride. There was no question that I would be sucked into its frothed flesh to suffer with all whom it had visited. Pain thrived in the skin of my heavily bandaged face, back and arms. Underneath the web of gauze I could feel the glaze of glass that was embedded within my skin. Even the slightest movement ground the glass' jagged edges deeper into my pores.

I felt as though my top layer of skin had been peeled back and replaced with a thorny quilt. Each prickly fiber shot pain throughout my body. After about ten minutes of being awake, the naked nerve endings on which pain traveled to my brain became overloaded. Pain was winning. It was gaining more control over me with each slight movement, with each passing second. There was more pain than there were routes to carry it. Pain had arrested so much control over me that I was limited to abrupt shallow breaths. No movement was too slight for it to return. I was imprisoned by it. Everything I did to try to escape only brought it nearer. The more I struggled to break free, the more entangled I became. I was helpless. All I could do was submit, "AAHH! It hurts!" I yelled. My skin contracted like a Boa, restricting me from saying another word.

I felt a familiar hand on my lips, "I know Tarique. I'm right here, don't worry.

"Ma?," I questioned the voice, but I knew the answer. "I know it hurts, but you'll have to be patient." Her words flowed smooth and lustrous as they left her lips. I believed she knew exactly how much pain I was in. Her voice answered the cries of every glass-filled pore on my body, covering me, then tucking me in for the night.

"You're cut up pretty bad. The doctors have had a time cleaning you up..."

"Where's Shandell?," I interrupted. I heard her inhale, filling her lungs with air to strum her vocal cords, but when she exhaled no words followed. She paused for a second.

"Ma, where is he? Is he okay? What's going on?!" Without giving her a chance to respond I exploded on her, "Where in the hell is he?!" and pain shot through me harder and faster than ever before, commanding me to be still, scolding me for my outburst. The beast that had guided me into the epitome of suffering seconds before, had returned to take me even deeper into its cold dark cave.

"Look Tarique, I understand there's a lot goin' on, but there ain't no need to talk to anybody in this room like that." I knew she was right, but apologizing wasn't at the top of my list.

"Well then, why can't somebody answer my goddamn question?"

Irritated and inches away from exploding herself, she captured her composure and said, "Look boy, I ain't got time for this shit."

Exhausted from fighting the pain, I pled, "Ma," (breath), "where," (breath), "is," (breath), "he?" .

"He didn't make it." I exhaled and the pain predictably answered the movement. Her statement filled me with an emptiness that no words could fill. The only sounds that followed were the hum of the machines and distant paging of doctors and nurses. She didn't say anything else. I heard her take two steps away from the bed and then gingerly sit on, what sounded like, a vinyl chair. Its smooth surface sounded off as it gave way to her tiny body. The chair crunched and moaned when she sat and then leaned back. Within seconds the chair welcomed her with an approving silence. The background hum continued, my mother and the chair remained silent as if they didn't want to burden any of my senses.

"Ha...," a voice said.

"Shh.." my mother interrupted.

"Who's there?! Ma' who's in here!"

"Tarique, calm down," she said with a healthy portion of frustration.

"Who is it then? Who in the hell just came in!?"

"Look Tarique, I told you to watch your Goddamn mouth. You're not gonna be talkin' to me like that. Shit." I heard her nudge the person towards me. She whispered, "Go ahead," to the stranger. The person didn't say a word at first. I could hear them walking nervously toward me.

"It's me Tarique." the voice trembled.

"Huh?" The voice was so faint and distant that, with all of the bandages around my head, I couldn't make it out.

"Bria." The voice replied. I exhaled with disgust and she flew out of the room.

My mother got up and the chair cracked and moaned, "Boy what in the hell is your problem!?"

"If it wasn't for her, I wouldn't be here and Shandell wouldn't be dead."

"Have you lost your Goddamn mind! That girl ain't done a damn thing wrong to nobody. She didn't asked to be raped and she didn't ask you to be fightin' nobody. All she done was be and the rest was up ta' ya'll."

"She didn't have to go with him outside. She knew he was drunk. She knew how he was."

"Look, I don't know what all happened at that little girl's party, but I do know that the last thing on Bria's mind was being raped and having the situation end up the way it did."

"Well then why'd she go with him?"

"Look boy, maybe you didn't hear me. I don't know what in the hell went on last night. All I know is what I see today. Shandell is gone. You just been taken off of the critical list and that girl was just released from the hospital herself a few hours ago."

"Huh?"

"Yah, you heard me. She was just released from HUP, (the Hospital of the University of Pennsylvania), and tha' first thing she did was to get her mother and father to bring her over here to see how you was doin'. She ain't even been home yet. The three of 'em sat here with me while you slept. Her mother and father had to leave to go to church and she stepped out for a second to go the bathroom before you woke up. The whole time she was here, all she did was apologize to everybody and cry. It ain't like she had to. She didn't do a damn thing to neither one of y'all."

I was upset and confused. Within fifteen minutes I had gone through more physical pain than ever in my life. I found out that Shandell was dead and that Bria had also been hurt badly. "How is she doin'?," I said, trying to make some sense of something.

"She's bad off. Three of her ribs are broken, along with her nose and she got cuts and bruises all over her. Her right eye is closed up and her lip..."

"All right, all right," I interrupted, "I hear you. So look at me!" I commanded, "I can't see. I can't move a muscle without pain shootin' all over my body. Man, I can't even breathe right and Shandell is dead. I'm real sorry to hear about her black eye. Maybe one day I'll even be able to see it."

"You just don't get it do you? Everybody lost this time. Ain't nobody better off than nobody else. Snooky lost her baby, I almost lost you and Bria has been raped and she thinks that all of the other shit is her fault!," when she finished she was yelling. Disgusted, she concluded, "Look, I've been up all night. I need some coffee and you need some rest. I'm gonna go get a doctor and some coffee, I'll be back in a little while."

I heard her moving away from my bed and then, I heard her leave the room, "Ma?.. MA!," I yelled and only pain answered. "Oh, so now you gonna leave me?" No one answered. Then, as loud as I could, "Maaa!!," pain shot through every millimeter of my body and for the first time, I cried. I don't know if it was one or all the things that were going on that made me cry, but the tears wouldn't cease until I ended up crying myself to sleep.

Monday morning I awoke to Bria. She stormed into my room and blew up at me. "You've got some damn nerve!" I was asleep. It took me a second to register who she was and what was going on. I was as bandaged as the day before, so I still couldn't see and it was hard for me to hear.

"Huh?"

"You heard me. You've got some damn nerve trying to make me

feel like all of this was my fault. The only reason I was at the party was because Shandell told me that you wanted to see me. Then, when I get there, you're kissing some slut. What was I supposed to do, join in?"

"So did that mean you had to go out and sleep with Shandell?"

"I was raped you selfish son-of-a-bitch! Raped! The last thing I wanted to do was to be with anyone in anyway."

"But you still went with him. You knew how Shandell was. Everybody knew how he was. If you was with him you was fair game." When the words came out, I knew that they were the wrong ones.

"Oh so that's what I am now, a game?"

"Did I say that?," too proud and too caught up to change the direction of the conversation.

"I don't know, did you? I don't know what you're saying Tarique, but you need to know that Your Boy, threw me to the ground and ripped my clothes off..."

I interrupted, "I don't want to hear this."

"And I didn't want to live it. Do you think I wanted a broken nose, three cracked ribs and..."

I interrupted her again, "I said I don't want to hear this!"

"No, but you need to hear it, see because what you don't know is that...," she stopped and I heard her start to cry. As the pause grew longer, the hum of the machines and the never-ending paging on the intercoms faded into silence. All that was left was the sound of Bria's tears gliding down her face.

"What's wrong wit' chu?!" I said, not wanting to show that I was fazed by her tears. There was no answer. Then I heard her walking in the direction of the vinyl chair. It welcomed her with a long moan followed by some creeks. I could imagine Bria doubled over in pain. Her body, the same one that used to do back hand springs in gymnastics, was now without the strength to stand erect. My voice lowered to a whisper, "Bre' what's wrong?," there was still no answer. I could hear her breaths skipping through her crushed ribs, making their way out of her twisted nose. "So what chu' cryin' for?"

"I wanted you to be the first Tarique." I swallowed. What went down was my pride. When it made it to the pit of my stomach, I nearly vomited a bucket of self-pity. She was a virgin. She told me that the reason she was one was that she wanted to make love to her husband, not have sex with a boyfriend.

"Bre'?" My voice cracked, because it wasn't used to carrying the weight of apologies. "Umm, Bre'?," my voice continued to crawl along. "I ah,...," each word was a timid step toward an apology. "Bre', I'm s...."

"What's goin' on in here?" I didn't hear my mother come in, I guess Bria didn't either. "Tarique, you better not have made this girl cry."

Bria politely laughed, "No Mrs. Oakman, I'm all right."

"You sure, 'cause I can still give him a beatin'." My mother liked Bria and on top of that, she was a clown. Any chance at making somebody laugh she took it. "He can't run from me now." Then she started in on some story about when I was little and how she used to have to chase me around the kitchen table to give me a beating. The two of them laughed like old friends.

I was in the hospital for the next month. I spent my days and nights in hot baths to soak the remaining glass out of my skin. The only visitors I had were my mother and Bria. All those people, whose voices were still horse from screaming my name at the championship at the game, had fallen silent. They had a new event to prepare for and a new hero. That event was a funeral and their new hero was Shandell.

Death was the birth canal through which the swarthy cloth of Shandell's earthly faults was washed away so that he could be dressed in the sanctity of divinity. When the papers came to ask people's opinion of him they'd say, "Everybody loved him, ...He was a good boy,... We're all surprised." Listening to them you could have easily thought his hands were nailed to the wooden planks of Karen's deck. The church people said, "He was summoned to serve a more noble calling." Shandell was reborn in death and when he returned to the Bottoms, he was drenched in the cleansing blood of the Creator.

He was to be buried Wednesday, three days after he died. During the two days of preparation, Bria would come in and tell me all about some of those fools out there. True, some people were upset because the community had lost another teenager. It is a tragedy to lose a child, because no child is expendable. But it is more tragic to neglect the truth, for any reason. Too many of them wanted someone or something to believe in and they found both in Shandell.

Some of the people who got dressed up on Sunday mornings called me Peter. These people who selectively remember the ten commandments, told stories of the three times I dissed Shandell. They had a nice story that chronicled it too. First, there was the time I didn't block for him. Then there was the time I didn't quit the team with him, and, the final betrayal was, when I sold him out for Bria. The older guys Shandell hung out with said that all Shandell ever did was try to do right by me. It got back to me that they said that, "If it wasn't for Sha Sha, Tarique wouldn't have even made the football team." Their favorite thing to say was, "That day in the gym Sha Sha almost died for him." Ottis was telling people that Shandell was the faster and stronger of us. "The one the colleges really wanted was Sha Sha, but the coach didn't like him."

Everything was my fault. So many people talked about me like a dog that I was beginning to lose count. The worst thing about it was that they either didn't know what they were talking about or they simply lied. It didn't bother me too much that all these people were talking about me, because I had already kicked them out of my life. What hurt was when they said, 'If he stuck by his side, Sha Sha would probably still be alive.'

Although Bria had friends at my school, she was pretty isolated from all of the drama. Chestnut Hill Academy had more white people than Woodstock. They had no idea what was going on in the Bottoms. The moon is closer to the sun than the chocolate city is to the vanilla suburbs in this town. But Bria didn't need to take the twenty-minute drive back to her neighborhood to get away from all of the rumors. She could have walked a few blocks in any direction. Going from one block to another in Philly can be like going to a different country. Although the big bad University of Pennsylvania practically shares the same zip code as us, you can believe that there aren't too many poor black folks walking around there. The Bottoms were the Bottoms, everywhere else was everywhere else.

Every time Bria came to visit I made her tell me everything they were saying. She hated to do it. She saw how it affected me. She knew that no one knew Shandell like I did. They knew 'Sha Sha.' Who was he? I lived with Shandell. They spray painted a memorial to 'Sha Sha' on an abandoned building on 34th and Haverford. I didn't need a picture, I had a lifetime of memories. Their memorial said his date of birth, the amount of career yards he rushed for and it had his picture.

I don't know what hurt Bria more, what they said about me or her. They called her a whore and said she'd always liked Shandell. They said that she deserved to be raped. They said she saw the party as an opportunity to finally get with him. She was a gold digger who messed with every guy on the team and guys on the team confirmed this. They told stories about the time she 'looked' at them at a party. They said that they could tell that she was dirty because of the 'way' she looked at them. Some of the guys on the team said that they had even tried to warn me about her, 'But his nose was wide open and there wasn't a thing we could do...and besides, if she didn't want it, why was she with him at that time of night?'

People said, 'Bria was the one who got between the Horsemen. Before her, they were tight.' They said that back then they couldn't tell us apart. Ottis said that, "She knew Tarique was on the football team, and that was it, she had to get some." One of the girls at my school who used to be cool with Bria said, "She didn't fool me, she wasn't all 'dat smart." I can't remember the girl's name, but she told people that Bria was even messing with one of her teachers and that's why she got such high grades.

My mother didn't fare too well under the neighborhood anger either. Somebody said that the reason she didn't have any men around was because she was a lesbian. Rumors were the least of my mother's concerns. She was trying to take care of her son and make a life for herself. She told me, "I ain't worried about those people, I'm about to move anyway." And move she did. Not long after the funeral she got a place in Mount Airy.

The most egregious misrepresentation of the truth happened when they talked about Snooky. She was praised for raising such a fine son. It didn't take long to find out that most of the people speaking on her behalf were addicts just like her. It's no coincidence that they were also church people, because what is church but an Alcoholic's Anonymous meeting? The question is, who in there is not hiding from some addiction? Who's not trying to find 'salvation' from their own shortcomings? They didn't need God, they needed to look in the mirror, but instead they'd rather pass judgment on us, and exalt a junky. They needed some justification for the terrible things they were doing to their bodies while their own children watched and raised themselves. They needed to justify their own life, otherwise the only other options they had were to see their life for how wrong it really was and then change it. That was too hard, so they decided to talk shit about us.

Snooky's girls said that it wasn't her fault she had to quit college. They knew she would've been somebody if she could've finished. These people where determined to make Snooky look good. The tragedy of Shandell's death gave those crazy people the forum to speak. They somehow found some justification for her ongoing participation in a fraternity party. "She was supposed to have a lot of men around," one of them said, "how else could she give her son a role model." They said, "If you want to see what happens when you don't have men around, just look at the killer Jennifer raised." Jennifer also raised the deceased, but that didn't matter.

As preparations for the big day continued, not a seat in the neighborhood's kitchens were empty. Nothing but straightening combs brewed on the stove. Lying in my hospital bed I could imagine the little girls sitting between their mother's legs getting their scalps greased. I knew the people around my block too well to forget that everybody had to look their best. This included the children. This event came at an awkward time. It was just before the holidays. People who were planning on attending had to make a difficult decision, 'Either I cut into the Christmas budget or I buy something I can wear on New Years' Eve.' It also came with little notice. This made it even harder to budget.

The funeral was on Wednesday, December 11, at 11:00 a.m. This meant that it wasn't long before checks came. People decided to spend the little money left over from their last check to get themselves hooked up.

The question on the streets became, 'So whachu wearin' to the funeral?' Nobody wanted to be outdone. The young men wore Stacey Adam's shoes and long thin ties. The women had leather skirts and rayon tops. Bria said the Chinese stores were packed. Wednesday morning the streets of the Bottoms were going to be filled with people who still had the store creases in their pants. When all you have are the clothes on your back, you'll spend all you've got to make them look like a million bucks. By the time everybody finished buying their clothes and getting their hair and nails done, most didn't have enough money left to buy flowers or a card.

For the older people, there were more left over rabbit fur coats than in a seventies' Blacksploitation film. Jheri still curled a few heads as his acidic juices burned hair into attention. The ruffle of plastic perm gloves could be heard for miles, while plastic bags were adorned like crowns. People had to keep their hair 'moist', regardless of what their hair wanted or was supposed to do. Touch ups were not to be taken lightly. Nobody wanted to leave the kitchen or the shop with less hair than they came in with.

Rev. Gibbs said it would be an honor to have an event of this size in his sanctuary. He knew that the host church would forever be known as 'the place where Sha Sha had his funeral'.

In 1987, we were in the midst of a terrible winter. The hawk had come and taken residence in the Bottoms. His talons had grabbed hold of the whole city and wouldn't let go. They say Black people don't like to be cold. That winter helped to prove that. The especially premature and harsh winter had cleared the streets in the days before the funeral. The bounty hunters, who killed for dead Presidents, had even come in from the cold. Even the most diehard corner crawlers had taken refuge inside. But this was different. The funeral was going to be a sight to see and nothing was going to stop these people from attending. Although it had snowed the night before the funeral and the temperature had dropped to near freezing, too much preparation had gone into this event for it to be called off. Everybody knew that under such harsh whether conditions hair do's had an abbreviated shelf live. They were determined to make sure everybody saw their hair before it was done. Borrowed clothes had to be returned and people had already taken the day off. In sum, the show must go on.

A few hours before the funeral, the snow stopped. It held its position long enough for the well groomed troop of Black people to march through the church's doors. A friend told Bria that the funeral was magnificent. She said that there was a band with seven trumpets who almost blew the roof off the joint. Everybody was shoutin' and clappin' and at least thirteen people said that during the service they could feel Shandell's presence within them. Ms. Emily and Mrs. Washington told everybody how they felt him touch them. They know that they didn't feel a damn thing. Those old geezers were 'touched' long before they dragged their saggy asses into the church that day.

The whole thing was choreographed better than a Michael Jackson video. In the front row there were twenty-four elders who, when they got their cue, bowed at the alter. These were the same convalescent cripples who wouldn't have aimed their drool at 'Sha Sha' while he was alive. But on that day, they jumped and shouted, or should I say swayed and moaned, like he was their own. I guess dying is quite an accomplishment, because in death Shandell became the gold friend of the neighborhood.

Lost in the 'celebration' were the genuine feelings of loss felt by so many. Mothers, fathers, sisters and brothers all shared the collective pain that comes from knowing and losing someone. There is no easy way to lose one of our own. We watch them grow and make mistakes. We want to believe that they will make better decisions when they get older, so we continue to support them. Most do. Most of the kids do grow up right. No, all of them don't go to college, but since when is that the only measure of success? Most, if they live long enough, are able to make it through whatever it is that they first encountered as a teen. Sure they will carry the children they've created with them, its no mystery that they will bare the marks of 'that night when they..', but most will come to add to the community. When their life is cut short, so too is their chance for redemption and a piece of our future.

The Window Pain

Poor inner city neighborhoods are saturated with two things, liquor stores and churches. Shandell's funeral had more than its share of well-dressed drunks. Inside the church it was hotter than Bermuda in August. Outside the snow again began falling, taking the temperatures below freezing with it. The winds picked up and howled, shaking the church's stain glass windows. Inside the worsening weather conditions went unnoticed as worshippers rose to the service's climax. The band played, the choir sang and the place shook. Even the sedate old 'Ah Lord' ladies were swept away by the frenzy of emotions. Banging and bouncing, swinging and swaying, screams came from every corner of the sanctuary. Nothing was dry. Not even the walls. Tears flowed endlessly. Hands were clapped raw. Voices were lost. Faster and faster, harder and harder, the message kept coming as testimony after testimony remembered Shandell David Eliab. Reverend Gibbs, the first preacher collapsed from a James Brownesque exhaustion. He was relieved by his more than capable backup, Assistant Pastor Simms, who grabbed the Bible from the falling Gibbs, pointed to the doors and commanded, "Let us take this child to his father!"

The band banged at a fatiguing pace for a few more minutes while people jumped and shouted the residue of the Holy Ghost out of their system. Others groped for their keys and started putting on their coats. When the first person made it to the door, the chill he felt traveled all the way back to the Elders in the front pews. The procession was frozen in its tracks. An invisible, impenetrable wall of weather was beyond the church's red wooden doors. Each jewel that fell from the sky glistened amid the mid-afternoon sun. Flakes floated carelessly to the ground, gently lying atop the ones that had fallen before. Like cotton, the snow settled on the black streets, its presence deadening the car horns and screams of summer in the Bottoms. The soundtrack of life to which we danced disappeared behind the winter's curtain. The snow fell steadily, silently. Its endless flow greeted the worshippers as they reached their cars. The chill that came with each flake jolted them back to earth. Moans of disapproval surfaced as the church emptied. The snow touched the attendee's faces like a child's cold fingers and then evaporated into an enchanting fog. Its steady flow calmed them and brought them back to the somberness of the moment. The snow politely tapped them and told them that the party was truly over, Shandell was dead.

Everyone got in their cars and drove off in unison. The long line of cars slithered through the streets like a mosaic iron snake. Most people followed the procession to the cemetery. Others broke off and went in separate directions. Many of them said they were concerned about venturing out into the cold of the cemetery because it would put them at risk of catching pneumonia. They had been dripping with sweat and they that said they 'knew' Sha Sha would understand their having to go home. While still others had different plans. They were going to celebrate, because they 'knew' Sha Sha would have wanted it that way. When they got home they toasted Sha Sha. Forty ounces were cracked open and the first sip was poured to the ground, for their fallen homie.

When the procession got to the cemetery, the once raucous crowd, didn't speak above a whisper, if they spoke at all. Sha Sha had been raised in the Highest. He'd been seated at the right of the Almighty. He was too massive to be lowered into the ground in a simple box. The chariot that would carry him the rest of his journey was majestic mahogany, with purple satin throughout, accented with polished brass. While the women cried and the preacher preached, men from the community took turns pulling clouds of dirt from the frozen ground and tossing them into the opening. The freed clumps of earth drummed on the vessel, christening it, as it began the last leg of its voyage home.

Reflections in the Window Pain
Chapter 7

The last leg of a journey is always the most difficult. It's the crossroads where exhaustion and elation meet.

Recovery was an arduous process. The month I spent in the hospital was followed by three weeks of healing as I awaited trial. My trial had to be postponed until February 21, 1988 at 9:00 a.m. because, even though I was out of the hospital, I still wasn't ready to stand trial. R. Gamila Goldstein was the public defender assigned to my case. I was charged with second degree manslaughter. Ms. Goldstein was Harvard educated and socially aware. Before she went to law school she worked in a youth detention center in Boston. When she moved to Philly for law school at Penn, she also received a degree in social work.

I first met Ms. Goldstein when I was in the hospital, still wrapped up like a mummy. I couldn't see what she looked like. The way she talked didn't give me any clue as to whether she was Black or white. Except for the teachers at my school, I hadn't met too many Jewish people. Her last name didn't mean anything to me. All I had to go on was a raspy voice that said words like "dude" and "ya'll" in the same sentence. She seemed more like a cross between a surfer and a B-girl, than she did a lawyer and a social worker.

My mother was worried about her at first. She hadn't had much contact with Jews before either and when she did they were her bosses. All she had ever been told was that Jews were money hungry and were only out for self. In a situation like mine, where I was facing five to fifteen years, she didn't want to have a lawyer who was only collecting a paycheck. We were in a bind though, so we didn't have much choice. My stay in the hospital had taken its toll on my mother not only emotionally but financially as well. She had limited health insurance. By the time I left, we were almost totally out of money.

Ms. Goldstein gained my mother's trust by first arranging emergency financial assistance. Then she set up a payment plan with the hospital. Getting my mother the assistance was no problem for Ms. Goldstein. She was trained in two fields to get people money. The problem was convincing my mother to take it. We hadn't been on welfare since about six months after we left my father. We needed it then because my mother didn't have any savings. Now that she was working two jobs, she couldn't rationalize being broke.

She was proud; too proud at times. She did whatever she had to do to stay off welfare. She even started talking about taking on a third job. She was already working close to sixty-five hours a week. The rest of her time she spent taking care of me. It didn't take long for her to realize that the third job was inconceivable under those conditions.

She had fallen behind on the bills when my condition grew serious. During that first week-and-a-half, my mother had to cut back on her night hours at Lee's Hoagies on 38th and Walnut. Minus that extra cash, we ended up in a deep hole. Ms. Goldstein knew that, regardless of what happened during and after the trial, my mother needed a place to stay. Therefore, she turned her legal briefs in for her social worker heart. She explained to my mother that the money she would be receiving was money from a system she paid into. The money she would be receiving was essentially from taxes the government had taken out of her paychecks. Ms. Goldstein told her that she had as much of a right to the assistance as she did to the police, army and street cleaners, because she paid for it.

It wasn't an easy sell, but it worked. Once my mother's living situation was stabilized, Ms. Goldstein began to concentrate on my defense. The prosecutor wanted to put me away for a long time. Ms. Goldstein said he liked putting Black people away for a long time. I was tried as an adult, because I was eighteen.

Ms. Goldstein suggested we cut a deal with him. She said

she'd ask him to come down to 3rd degree involuntary manslaughter, because of the severity of the injuries I'd sustained and because I hadn't intended to kill Shandell. I had over one hundred and fifty stitches on my head, neck, arms, hands and back. She wanted the trial to be as quick as possible for two reasons. The first reason was that she felt the sooner the trial was over the sooner I could start serving my sentence. Ms. G, as she liked to be called, said she wanted me to hurry up and get on with my life. The second reason was for my mother. Ms. G took a liking to her. She respected her spirit and drive. She always called my mother Ms. Oakman and she never made a move without consulting her first. She and my mother had gotten close. Ms. G knew all of this was crushing her. She wanted to save her as much additional grief as possible.

Bria was there through my recovery and trial. She was a great help to my mother. There were times when she and Ms. G used to force my mother to go off by herself. In the meantime she and Ms. G combined to create a schedule to make sure I was never alone. They'd rent movies for me, change my bandages and generally do whatever they needed to do to help me physically and mentally. They worked very hard to keep my spirits up. Sometimes when my mother was out, Ms. G would leave Bria and me alone. We'd just talk, but it felt so good to talk to Bre. She made it all make sense. She listened to me when I droned on and when I cried, and there were many times when I cried, she just let me do it. No strange looks, just love and understanding. She made me feel like a man, even when I was helpless.

Ms. G's plan worked exactly as she hoped it would. The prosecutor agreed, I pled no contest and on March 16, 1988, I was delivered to Graterford Correctional Facility to start my minimum five year term.

While I was going through rehabilitation and the trial, Stacey had the baby. It was a girl. She named her Sha Sha Shantique Eliab. We are always making up names. She and Snooky were inseparable during those first few months. They paraded their little project princess around the city. The infant was always on tour. "Oh she looks just like Sha Sha ... I bet she'll be good in sports too," people said. Infants don't look like anybody except other infants. All babies look the same.

That's what makes them so cute. Any baby that looks like an adult can make you wince. Although it might seem like it takes a lifetime to get as ugly as some people get, the fact is that the ugly process starts later.

They started to split when Snooky found out that Stacey was pregnant again. They got into a custody battle that lasted a year. A drug addict and a slut fighting to get a baby, could there possibly be any more losers in this one? There may not be a more woeful situation. They didn't want little Sha Sha. The poor little baby was nothing more than a thing to them. A prize to be won. Snooky and Stacey were not as interested in raising a child as they were in making sure the other person didn't win. Stacey ended up getting the little girl. By the time Sha Sha was two she was taken into foster care. Somebody called the Department of Human Services on Stacey because she had been seen going to the store and leaving the child at home alone. DHS offered to give custody to Snooky, but she couldn't be found, it was rumored that she had finally checked into rehab.

Not long after I got here I realized that Graterford is a who's who of the neighborhood. Hi-C is here, not for beating 'Shanna though. He shot a guy at the Purple Palace and almost killed him. If you let him tell it, the guy was lucky, but everybody else said that the gun just went off. Apparently the guy had Charles in a headlock and was pounding the hell out of his face. Somehow as the guy beat Charles nearly unconscious, Charles' gun fell out. Charles grabbed it. A struggle ensued and it went off, hitting the guy in the chest; the bullet came out of his back. It punctured his lung, but the ambulance got there in time to save him. O.D. is in here too.

When I first got here a few of the other inmates tried to test me, but there wasn't a thing small on me. Even though I hadn't worked out in a few months, I was still 6'2" and I weighed over two and some change. I got into a few fights, but I never had too much trouble. Another reason I escaped a lot of trouble that most young boys who end up there was because some of the other inmates had heard what I was in for. Having a body underneath you garners a certain amount of respect, especially if it was your boy. Some people see it as, 'Here's a person who will kill anybody'. Although that wasn't the case with me, it served its purpose.

As I got settled in during those first few months, my biggest problem became boredom. Most people fill their time with card games for phone time and cigarettes. I don't smoke. Because of the 'endless' list of activities here, I ended up spending most of my time staring out my window thinking about what it used to be like just a few months before. Sometimes it felt like the only thing I did was think. And think and think and think.

I thought about everything and everybody. I'd spend hours before I went to sleep thinking about all sorts of people and places I'd seen and been. I thought about my mother, Shandell, and Bria; mostly Bria. I even thought about people I'd only met a few times. Bria wrote me regularly. Reading her letters conjured up thoughts and memories of people and places that, when I was on the outside, I took for granted. On the inside there were no thoughts too small to take me away. Her letters invited visions of what it was like on the outside to leap the barbed wire fence, squeeze through the bars and dance in my head as I lie there at night.

Every piece of the outside world became precious. Memories swept me up in their intoxicating glow and took me to a time when I was growing up. The memories smacked like furiously twirled double dutch rope, giggled like "hide and go get" and flowed like open water plugs. Thinking about what it used to be like on the outside allowed me to escape for a few minutes. Then, as memories sometimes do, these thoughts would bring me full circle. Back to my cell and my incarceration.

"Why are you with me?" During my first summer in Graterford, Bria came to visit me every week. It was the summer before she went off to Penn. She'd come and stay the full hour and she knew before she got there that she was going to get the same question. The only thing different about this conversation from one visit to the next, was the day it occurred.

"Because I love you Tarique."

"So. What does that have to do with why you're with me?"

"Because you're a good person," she'd say almost before I finished my question.

Steve Perry

"What's so good about me? I killed my best friend. I'm in jail for a long time. And I look like shit." I have a scar that goes from below my right eye, over the bridge of my nose and extends to my left cheek. I honestly couldn't understand what she saw in me. I figured if she was really looking at me, she'd see who I really was. I came to the conclusion that she had no idea of who I really was. Maybe this was because all she knew was what I'd allowed her to see. I knew what I was capable of doing. I knew the thoughts that went through my head about being with other women. She obviously had no idea how close I'd be to making those thoughts reality. If she knew this, she would have left me a long time ago. I tried to tell her, but she wouldn't listen. Then again, I wanted her to know, but I didn't say it point blank. I knew I loved Bria, but I didn't know what that meant.

She had the world at her feet and I was gum on the bottom of her shoe. I sincerely wanted to make our plan work. We'd go to college, graduate and get married. In my heart that's the way I wanted it to go, but it was another part of my anatomy that told me otherwise.

I felt her love, but tried to run away from it. As much as I didn't want to, I'd fallen absolutely in love with Bria. My warnings of who lies behind the eyes she said she adored were feeble attempts at disclosing how I really felt. She knew how much I loved her. That's why she patiently answered my insecurities like a mother answering the endless questions of a child.

I didn't know what she saw in me. I told her what she was looking at was what she wanted to see. I warned her that eventually she was going to see me for who I was. She wouldn't listen. Every time she came to visit, I felt as if somebody was slowly pouring warm water on me from head to toe. Its smooth consistency traveled the length of my body and embraced me. It was love. It was a child blowing bubbles on a sunny summer afternoon, discovering the delicate flesh of a rose, dancing and laughing, sitting on a stoop marveling at a spore in flight. Its complete complexity maneuvered through my crass existence, sending goose bumps down my arms and putting butterflies in my stomach.

I couldn't wait for her to get here and when she got here I didn't want her to leave, but while she was here I didn't know how to act. I couldn't say, 'Hey baby, I'm so glad to see you," I had to say, "Why you always wearin' shit that shows off your shit to everybody?" Nope, I couldn't do the adoring affectionate boyfriend thing in person, but then I'd turn around and let my pen be guided every night by the glib rhythm of my heart. Its melody would serenade its empress with melodies that told stories of a time when they'd again be together. Its steady flow pounded a reminder that when winter's frost dissipated, it will take with it its baron landscape exposing, our love, because spring is inevitable.

While Bria was getting ready for her first year at Penn I was trying to adjust to life in a cage. We were both in transition. "I know you gonna end up screwin' somebody else when you get to school."

"Whatever Tarique. There's no sense in me saying it again so I won't, you're right I am gonna 'screw' somebody else."

"See, I told you! I knew 'dat shit! I knew as soon as I got locked up you was gonna mess with somebody else."

"I guess it's time for me to leave...," she said as she stood up.

"No, no, no...," I grabbed her hand to stop her, a guard stood up and I let go. "C'mon Bre', I just don't know what else to say." I wanted to tell her everything I was thinking; my fears and my feelings. I didn't know how. I wanted to give her everything, but I was chained to my decision to act out of aggression. If she'd told me she wanted the moon, I would've gotten a step-ladder and unscrewed it like a bulb.

She looked at me and said, "Say what you feel." She knew me better than I thought. She used to tell me that it was my eyes that always told on me. So I looked down as if to say I couldn't let her know what I was feeling and she got up again.

"ALL RIGHT, ALL RIGHT, ALL RIGHT! I love you."

"Say it like you mean it," she said with a half grin and raised eyebrows.

"I love you! Damn how many other ways you want me to say it?"

"Now was that so hard?" she said with a smile.

I started laughing too, "Whatever."

When school started she got a lot of work. I didn't press her for her time. I still wrote her every night, but I understood when she didn't always write back. She was meeting new friends, learning about biology, adding and subtracting numbers that looked like letters and getting more beautiful each day. I kept a picture of her in my shirt pocket at all times. When she was able to visit she'd tell me all about her new friends and the things she was learning. It hurt to hear her talk about a world I couldn't experience. I mean, I was happy for her, but I hated to hear every word.

About a month after school started Bria came to visit and she was telling me about the best places to find quiet when she wanted to study. The conversation was going well. She talked without stopping and I added nods from time to time. I was so happy to see her that, at times, I didn't hear what she was saying because I was too busy smiling and watching her mouth. I was out of it, but I wanted her to keep talking. So I asked her a question about Penn's football team and she started her answer with, "Well, Byron said.." I interrupted, awakened by a man's name.

"Who's 'Byron'?" I snapped.

"Tarique, he's just this guy from my Intro to Engineering class who plays on the football team. Everybody in engineering is male and white or Chinese, but he's Black," she smiled and assuredly patted my hand.

"Look, I don't want you hanging around a bunch of nigga's."

"Everybody in my class is a male, so I have no choice." Her face straightened up. She folded her arms, leaned back in her chair and shook her head, "Byron said you were going to act like this when I mentioned his name and he was right."

I jumped out of my seat, "Who the fuck is he!" a guard looked over at us.

"Look Tarique, get used to it, because he's my friend and I'm not quitting school because you're jealous," and then she got up and left.

I stayed up all night. First, I was pissed, 'Who does she think she is?' By around 4:00 a.m. I cooled down and realized I had overreacted. I wrote her a letter apologizing for the way I acted. From then on, when she came, she'd talk about school, this 'Byron' clown and whatever the hell else was going on. She'd talk about studying late and the two of them going to each other's rooms. She knew I hated what the two of them were doing, but she made it clear that if I gave her grief, she wasn't going to put up with it. That's why I smiled and acted interested or changed the subject.

On December 18, 1988 Bria came to visit. It was the last day of her exams and all the students were going home soon. We talked for forty-five minutes about her exams, her plans for break and the next semester.

"How's ya' boy?" I sarcastically asked. She hadn't mentioned his name the entire time. I thought I'd point it out.

"He's okay," was all she said.

"What's wrong?"

She looked me straight in the eyes, "I'm gonna miss him over break."

"WHAT! So what 'chu sayin'? Y'all fuckin'!"

"Not yet."

I sat back in my chair, put my hands over my face, ran my fingers through my hair, put them on the table on top of each other and exhaled. I looked at her. I couldn't say a word. There were none to be said. I again put my hands over my face, ran my fingers through my hair, put them on the table on top of each other and exhaled. I shook my head and smiled with disbelief. She didn't hang her head. She just looked at me like it was no big thing.

After about four or five seconds of silence she said, "I think I should go."

"Huh," I half laughed, as if to say 'That's a good idea'.

That was the last time I ever saw Bria Ghana. She kept in touch with my mother for a few months after, but that stopped too. Spring never came.

For the next two weeks I barely ate, never slept and spent any time I could in my cell alone, sometimes crying. Before I met Bria, I didn't even know if I could cry. I didn't cry when mother used to get beat down, when we left my father and it took me a while to do it when Shandell died, but when Bria hurt me, and eventually left, I cried effortlessly.

My mother came to see me during those two weeks. She'd let me go on and on about what Bria had done to me. I talked non-stop about what a no good witch she was and how I didn't care what happened to her. By the end of the second week I'd lost almost twenty pounds, my eyes were blood shot and my face was drawn, "You look a mess Tarique."

"Well how am I supposed to look?'

"Look boy, you just turned 19, you got the rest of your life to live. I'm sure it hurts, but you ain't doin' a damn thing for nobody by doin' this to yourself." My mother was irritated with me, which pissed me off.

"Why you mad at me? I ain't do nothing to you."

"Tarique, I liked the girl too, she was cute, smart, the whole nine, but hey, she had to do her thing, 'see ya'," she made a hand gesture like she was saluting. "It's over. Killing yourself ain't gonna bring her back."

"You just don't understand. You and my father ain't neva' loved each other so it wasn't no thing for you to leave."

"You've got a lot of damn nerve or maybe you jus' lost your mind, 'cause you don't know what in the hell you're talkin' about, but I can say this, it's always been me and you and that's the way it's gonna be for a long time! I'm the only woman who eva' did a damn thing for you. You need to get that shit through your head and start respecting me!" She picked up her stuff and walked out. All my life I'd never mentioned the day we left, but I was mad. I thought I'd throw it back in her face. She was hurting me when she was telling me to move on. Right or not, it hurt. I wasn't thinking, and I didn't care how much I hurt her, because she wasn't caring about how much she was hurting me. I never saw her that mad. She meant the world to me and I made her feel worthless.

That conversation with my mother hit home, but it didn't change my behavior. I still wasn't getting enough sleep or eating. My face had more bags than a nursing home and I was weak. After over two weeks of under-eating, it became difficult to hold down the food when I tried to eat. Even before Bria broke up with me, I ate alone. That didn't change. I sat at the end of a table or at a table by myself. One night at dinner I heard, "Yo, who sittin' here?" The voice rattled my tray. He didn't yell, but his voice was so deep that it made Barry White sound like a soprano. I looked up from my peas and all I saw was a waist. I lifted my head to about seventy degrees and I saw a chest, at about one hundred and thirty degrees I saw the biggest blackest man I'd ever seen. He was so big and black that he had two shadows and both of them were lighter than him. He had scars all over his face and he had a thick gray mustache. The hair on his lip was the only hair on his entire head. The more my head tilted back, the more my mouth opened.

By the time my eyes met his, my mouth was wide open. "Is anybody sittin' here?," his voice rumbled again like a convoy of eighteen wheelers.

With my mouth still wide open, I shook my head and said, "Huh, huh." He sat down with his tray and the table squealed under him. I have never been scared of anyone or anything, especially not another man, but when I looked down at the fork in my hand it was shaking. I dropped it and put my hands under the table.

A minute had passed and I wanted to run, leaving my tray and anything else behind me, but my knees wouldn't stop knocking together. He stood nearly 6' 8" and weighed over four hundred pounds. The whole time he sat across from me I kept looking down, like I was paying attention to my food. I was too scared to look at him.

"Love's a bitch ain't it?" Out of nowhere his words drummed me out of my trance. I looked up at him with my forehead twisted, as if to ask 'How'd you know?' I never told anybody about me and Bria or anything for that matter.

"Yeah, I know what 'chu goin' thu," the voice continued and then he went into a story about how he was married with five kids before he got locked up. "I had everything in her name so it wouldn't get took by the cops." He used to sell drugs. A lot of drug dealers did this. "She came up here one day and told me it was over, 'cause she wanted to marry my boy." He'd told his best friend to look out for his wife while he was locked up. He set his friend up with some money he had stashed away and he promised him more when he got out. Apparently his boy did take care of her real good because, "Now that nigga' is fuckin' my wife and he got my kids callin' him daddy." He told me he could 'see in my face' what I was going through. He remembered how everybody used to tell him to get over his ex. He said they didn't understand. "If yo' dog dies, you can't jus' git anotha' one. Life ain't like 'dat." We spent the whole dinner talking about "love" and over the next couple of weeks we got real cool. After a while we left love to the lovers and branched off into other subjects.

His name was Muggie and we had a lot in common. Neither one of us talked much and we liked to spend most of our time by ourselves. He was from the projects in North Philly. We'd both eaten government ripened cheese and canned ham. He was in his forties. I'd ask him about how it was when he was growing up. For months he told me stories about his life. He told me about the times when he could feel the warmth emanating from the brown skin of the community. He said that they used to have more parties than Hugh Hefner. Back then everybody looked out for each other and there was such a thing as family. One day when Muggie started to tell me a story he stopped. We'd become good friends, spending most of our time together, but I'd never seen him look at me the way he did. When he continued he said, "I'll tell you 'bout tha' back in tha' day if you teach me how to read." Even without working hard I did pretty well in school. During our conversations I'd told him how I'd intended on going to Temple. I immediately said yes, but my heart dropped. I couldn't believe this forty something year old man, with five kids and fifteen grand kids, couldn't read a lick. I couldn't believe that a man who was able to teach me so much had never been taught to read. He told me he wanted to know how to read, so that when he got out he'd be able to read to his grandchildren. He stuck out his hand and we shook on it.

Ever since Muggie started getting better at reading, he wanted to read everything. He didn't care if it was the paper or a bumper sticker he wanted to read and his favorite subject was, as he would say, "our people." Talking with him was the first time I ever looked at my community. It was the first time I took notice of the place and people that gave birth to me. All my life it was me, Shandell, football and girls.

Now I was the only thing left. For the first time something outside of girls and football was important.

Muggie loved to read and I loved teaching him. It passed the time and made me feel good. I felt like I was doing something worthwhile with myself. When he went into the library and came out with a book , he was like a child asking his mother to buy him something at the store, he'd ask, "Can we read 'dis one?" I loved his enthusiasm. One of the first books he picked out was The Autobiography of Malcolm X. It took us a year to read, but he never gave up. Through Muggie's stuttered words and Malcolm's hazel eyes, I started to see the sickness, not only our community, but the ones that fed off of ours. As I watched a grown man grapple with words like "ought" I realized that poverty distorts people's perception of reality, which can make them insane. For Muggie to grow up thinking that hustling is more important than reading is an example of this insanity. When you spend too much time draped in poverty your values burn like tiles on a space shuttle during re-entry. Muggie's inability to decipher the written word showed me that he alone could not have created this situation. He had help from outsiders who authored his living conditions and who still keep people like him in his place. These people suffer from the same delusion. The outside world, through their inaction to help us change the way we lived, had taken a positive action towards allowing the conditions to continue. When the suburbs screw the ghettoes, the ghettoes give birth to people like Muggie and me. When they feed off our substandard living conditions, they end up malnourished. Muggie and Malcolm joined hands to show me that people who feed on death will choke on its repugnant odor and bile taste.

Reading books with Muggie opened my world. From the books, magazines and newspapers we read, I learned of the struggles of our people. Together we learned how the waters of the Atlantic were muddied with the blood of millions of brown people. Before we started reading together, I had no idea of the extent to which the Atlantic Ocean's cool salt water air was saturated with the stench of death or how many lives were lost in the tangled matrix of slavery. The lost lives were calculated in millions and their people's wretched condition was seen as a collective, giving no respect to individual lives lost.

Teaching Muggie to read helped me to see the importance of putting books in hands once stained gray with gun powder, and desire in the hearts of those who couldn't see life beyond the dilapidated structures that housed them. Working with him ignited a fire within me to work with others like him and me. I couldn't wait to get out of jail to help others. My dream was to graduate from college and then go on to teach. Then I will be able to watch as the community members silently applaud with a nod or grin of affirmation as another one of their own slowly passes by them, as if they are on a float in a parade, on their way home from college break.

Muggie believed in me like Bria used to. He only knew I played football because I told him. To him, I wasn't a Horsemen. "You my teacher, lil' bro," he'd say with a huge grin. But to me, he was my teacher. He taught me more than he'd ever know. He showed me I can, no matter what. After a year of working with Muggie, I decided to work with other inmates so that the storm of ignorance would be reduced to a delicate summer breeze and never again will a 'teacher' have to be taught to read by his 'pupil'.

Teaching gave me something I never had before, a concern for others. It was who I was, not just what I did. Before I started teaching I'd spent 19 years of my life ruled by self-indulgence. Nothing and no one could stop me. Working with Muggie gave me a purpose, a life. Now when people saw me they'd say, "Tha's the teacher," never had a nickname felt so good.

Before I started teaching other inmates to read I consulted Muggie. I wanted to know who I should get with first, the older guys or the younger ones. He told me I needed to get with the older brothers first. He said, "If you git them straight, then the young ones will follow. 'Dem young boys all wanna be a part of somethin', but 'dey don't belong to nothin'." A whole bunch of the young brothers come in here and discover Allah and want to 'join' the Muslims. Finding God ain't hard when there isn't a damn thing here but men and bars.

Muggie told me that, "Too many of 'em can't even read tha' tombstones of the people they kill. Dey been poor for so long that they gave up tryin' to make their conditions better."

Everybody has a need to make sense of their conditions. In the process, some people get tired of making sense of it and try to change the conditions under which they live. Others also get tired, but they stop trying and start to justify the conditions they live under. This justification soon mutates into glorification. The result is that being 'Poor, Broke and Lonely, an Old Dirty Bastard or Nigga's With Attitudes', becomes cool.

Me and Muggie talked all the time about the songs we heard portraying the ghetto like it's OZ. It ain't. It's a place where too often people are born to die. All these rappers talked about growing up in the "hood" when the only hood they've been in was attached to a sweatshirt. For those who have, as soon as they make a little money they run like roaches to the suburbs.

Every day we welcomed another of our most promising young leaders to Graterford. He's returning to the shackles and prison bunk that were prepared for him at birth. At Muggies suggestion I started talking to the young brothers when they came in. I soon found out that they were not dumb. It didn't take me long to see that the reason they were here was their inability to resist making bad decisions. This had to do with the degree of their access to their true self. The bottom line was they didn't know who they were, so they were doing whatever to fit in, to belong, to connect to some one or something because they weren't connected to their family or themselves. When I asked them who they are they'd tell me where they're from, 'Norf Wes!'

I had to get my GED in here, but I made sure I got it. Hell is a long way to go to get a message, but the devil is a good motivator. It wasn't easy to convince these young boys that twenty one is not too late. It took a genuine belief that they really could make it. I always told them that my belief in them stems from being that same kid whose cheeks pressed against the same bars and dreamt of going to college.

Before I was able to convince them to let me teach them to read I had to establish a trust with the young men for whom trust had been harder to come by than decent living conditions. I knew where they were coming from, because my heart never left where

159

they resided. I too have seen the vacant shells that once housed proud families, breathed life into the crack pipes. Hopelessness once dwelled within me, but it had since been cast aside.

Trekking through life in a cage brought me great treasures as it had robbed me of the most precious of all commodities, time. Each day I was locked up took away from me the heaven that is the hope of living. Living in a cage is a hopeless life. Through teaching I was given a chance to hope.

Six months after I started teaching other brothers to read, my class grew to an average of eight students and it's been this way for the past three and a half years. None of this would have been possible without Warden P. Vaughan. Although he was tough, he was one of the most compassionate people I'd ever met. He and Muggie were the first Black men to just talk to me. He was never one to tell me how bad I had to be or pushing some forty down my throat. He cared. When I needed books for a workshop he'd give me ones from his own home library. There were even times when he'd buy a book for me and tell me he'd had it lying around the house, but it was obviously new.

Warden Vaughan was all I ever wanted in a father and a friend. I respected him more than I've ever respected another man and with his help I was able to answer a lot of questions that had been floating around in my head. He confirmed what Muggie told me about my ability to teach.

He told me I am talented and he encouraged me to pursue it, and while I in here, he made me practice. Even when I didn't feel like teaching, he made me do it. He told me that I needed to teach as much as the other inmates needed to learn. Warden Vaughan said, "Pay attention to your students, because sometimes they will teach you more about yourself and life than you could ever teach them." He demanded that I stay ahead of them. "When your information becomes obsolete, you do too." This was why I read everything I could get and through my readings, I learned a lot about teaching, other people, history and myself. One thing I learned is that after I get out of Graterford Prison, I'm not going back to the prison I left. I have outgrown the city. There is nothing appealing about living on top of people, surrounded by cement and bars. Dealing with the haunting feeling of worrying about somebody who's always ready to take my life, because they have no life of their own, is not what I saw in my future. Living like this had been my punishment, it makes no sense to pay rent in order to be punished again.

When I got out of prison I waned to be in a place where everywhere I looked there was grass and enormous trees whose fingers reach to the heavens. I wanted to live in a place like Maine, because roots don't grow in cement. To stay ahead of the inmates in my workshops I'd read parts of the encyclopedia. This is where I was introduced to the New England states. The more I read about them, the more I wanted to be there. I'd become obsessed with that part of the country. Maine was especially interesting. I'd been reading everything I could get my hands on about its beautiful rolling hills and breath-taking change of seasons from summer to fall.

I'd decided that Maine would be the womb that would give my family more than birth. It would pack my children's lunch boxes full of the essentials they would need as they traveled on throughout the school of life.

I will never forget the lessons I learned as I journeyed through this cement sin, but my heart will one day beat in harmony with the mighty pine trees and gentle breeze, in Maine. I couldn't wait to live up river in the place that would spawn my new lessons. When I got there I'd continue the work I'd started here.

Through Shandell's death I'd been born into a new world, but my first steps were on scared legs. It was an emotional stroke that forced me to start all over. The way I used to live robbed me of exploring my full humanity. My life, as I knew it, was over. There has been a death. The fire that raged that night at Karen's party was the catharsis. I couldn't have envisioned my capacity to grow. Now that I'd shed the skin I wore as a self centered little boy, I was able to take on the exterior I needed to become a complete man.

With less than a month left on my sentence, I started to get phone calls from my father. He said he wanted me to put him on the visitor's list. I hadn't seen or heard from him since the day we were cleaning up after my parents' fight. I couldn't have cared less if I ever saw him again, but Muggie and Warden Vaughan said maybe I should hear him out. They said maybe my father had something to say worth hearing. I still wasn't sure. This was the same man who caused my mother and me incredible pain. I kept asking myself 'what in the hell would be the purpose of me talking to him?'

After he started calling, I wondered if mother would be mad at me for talking to him. She hadn't seen him in a long time either. After they finalized the divorce he was gone. It took me a while before I asked her about how she'd feel about him visiting. Actually, three weeks went by between his first call and when I finally asked her. "Whatever," was all that she said and then she left it up to me.

Muggie, Warden Vaughan and my mother were all cool with me seeing him. I was at least curious about what he had to say. So I told him to come on up. I told him it was okay to visit and he said he'd be here after work on Friday. Over ten years had passed. I'd been wondering what he looks like and if that'll be what I'm going to look like when I get to be his age. I wanted to know what he had been up to, but most of all I wanted to know why, now, he wanted to see me. A few years back, I'd heard he moved to Dover, Delaware right after my mother left him. That was about all I knew or wanted to know about him at the time. I've hated him for what he did to my mother and there were many times I wanted him dead. But I convinced myself that if my mother was over it, then I should start to let it go too.

He came that Friday. He even got here early. His face lit up when I came into the room, "Hey buddy!" he excitedly said as he stuck out his hand for me to shake. I did. That whole telephone and glass partition thing, that's on TV, it isn't what I have to deal with. I only had forty-five minutes. I'd planned out everything I was going to say and I wanted to get past the bullshit.

We sat down and he spoke first. "I heard what happened between you and 'dat boy. I didn't realize how big it was 'til 'bout a year ago. I ain't really been in touch wit' nobody in Philly in a while. Ya' know what I'm sayin'?" he kind of laughed. I just looked at him. 'How strange it was to see him,' was the thought that kept going through my head.

"So what's up? Why'd you want to see me so bad?" I asked with no expression on my face or response to his earlier statement. I wasn't in the mood for jokes. I wanted answers.

"Well, I ain't seen you in so long and I jus' wanted to see how you was doin'."

"I'm chillin'." He laughed. "So, you married?"

"Naw, after me and yo' moms broke up, I jus' been by myself. You know she's the only woman I eva' loved."

"What about that lady that you said you used to work with at UPS?" I snapped.

"Aw, she wasn't nuttin'. She was jus' a trick and that was a million years ago."

"You told me somethin' serious went down that night though, but you never finished."

"Sex ain't serious."

"It is when you're married and you have it with somebody who ain't your wife."

"Yeah."

"But you made it seem like more than that. So what's up? I'm 'bout as grown as I'm gonna get. You said you wanted to talk to me, so let's talk; and you can leave the bull shit at the door." He looked at me for a second and scrunched his face. His expression told me that he could see I was serious.

He stopped smiling. "If you really want to know, I'll tell you. Like I told you back 'den, she thought she was all 'dat and I jus' wasn't down wit' chasin' no stuck up bitches, 'specially since your moms was already about to have you. So one night when I was at the Purple Palace, she started gettin' close to me...," I interrupted him and reminded him I only had forty-five minutes and already knew that part. He skipped ahead in the story.

"That night we had sex and a few weeks after 'dat she told me she was late."

"So, she was pregnant?" I said, still pushing the story along.

"That's what she said." I looked at him. I could not understand this man. He had a pregnant woman at home, who he

163

claimed to love, and he was out screwing some other woman.

"So what happened?"

"She had it," he said matter of factly.

"Did you take care of it?"

"Hell no! I didn't even know if it was mine." he was aggravated. "She said it was, but how was I 'posed to know 'dat shit?" With every new word, with each passing second, this man looked less familiar.

"What did she have?"

"A boy."

"What did she name him?"

"I don't know and I don't care. I don't even know if the shit was mine. Why is we talkin' 'bout this mess anyway? I ain't come all the way up from Dover to talk about somebody I ain't seen in all mos' twenty years."

"What was her name?"

"I don't know, Sandy or somthin'. Tarique why is we talkin' 'bout this mess anyway?"

"Sandy what?"

"Sandy somethin'. I don't know her last name," he was getting pissed, but I didn't care. "All I know was 'dat she turned into a fiend after she had tha' baby." And then, as if he had thought of the answer to the *Jeopardy* 'Daily Double', "OH! They used to call her Snooky, that's right!. People used to call her Snooky."

My heart dropped, I couldn't breathe, "What?!," I yelled as loud as I could.

"What's wrong wit 'chu?" he said.

I exploded, "That was Shandell's mother, your son was named Shandell! You said yourself that she wouldn't mess wit' nobody else at UPS, so who the fuck else's baby could it have been?" Everybody looked over at me.

"Who the hell is Shandell?"

"You goddamn idiot. Shandell was my friend who died. He fuckin' lived with me and ma' for over five years you asshole. He's the reason you're visiting me in a prison."

"Look boy, you watch the way you talk to me, I'm still your

father."

"Man, fuck you. A father is a man, and you ain't been a man a fuckin day in your life."

He jumped up and started pointing his finger at me. "You betta' watch how you talk to me boy! I'll get in that ass.."

I jumped to my feet and said in an even tone, with my teeth clenched, "You left a boy on the stoop cleaning up that glass, so you better sit your ass down before I take what's left of you manhood, bitch!" We were pointing in each other's face. Three guards immediately came and grabbed me. They threw my hands behind my back and started to cuff me. I didn't put up a fight, "I'm cool, I'm cool, jus' get this punk ass nigga outta my face before he gets hurt." The guards asked him to leave and they took me back to my cell.

Over the past five years I had been able to get to a place where I could cope with Shandell being gone, but this fool opened up the whole thing all over. Now, more than ever, what happened ripped at my insides. His death tore at everything I am. Shandell, my brother, was dead. How could that bastard have done this to us?

The incident with my father cost me my visitation privileges for a week. Warden Vaughan didn't really get in my stuff for the whole thing. He was pretty cool. He called me into his office and asked me to tell him what had happened. I told him every detail, down to how the guards had to restrain me before I hurt him. I told the Warden how much of a shock this was and how I've never felt worse in my life.

He listened to me go on for about ten minutes, like he always did, and then he said, "So." I looked up at him to see if he was talking to somebody else, but then he said it again, "Yeah I said it, so what?" I couldn't believe it. I thought to myself, 'Vaughan knows me. He has seen how I've turned around since I've been in here. He is the main reason I was not going to have to serve out the rest of my bid. Now here he was acting just like those niggas on the corner who think that they're too cool to cry or to be hurt.' I was bewildered. Then I thought, 'how could he', but I didn't say a word.

"Did you not hear what I said Mr. Oakman?" Did he really want me to answer him? I couldn't believe Warden Vaughan was treating me like this.

"Warden Vaughan, if you're gonna punish me, then do it, 'cause I got better things to do than sit here." He laughed.

"You are in prison son, you ain't got a damn thing to do but try and find a new way to iron your shirt and lie about how many 'bitches' you got waiting for you when you get out. All you've got is time Mr. Oakman." He folded his arms and leaned back in his chair waiting for me to say something. But what was there to say? He knew as well as anyone, even better, what Shandell meant to me. He knew everything we used to do, even down to the two girls we got caught with in my mother's house. Where was he going with this? Was it funny to him that I just found out that the person I killed was my brother?

There was an extended silence and then he leaned forward, put his forearms on his desk and said, "Does this make him any less dead?" I still could not believe him and at that point I saw no need to talk to him, because, as far as I was concerned, he didn't have shit to say.

"Mr. Oakman do you hear me talking to you?"

"Yeah, but you ain't sayin' nothin."

"What do you want me to say son? The two of you shared everything. He was the most important person in your life for most of your life. You loved him with the intensity of the sun, so what difference does it make that you shared the same father? A brother is not something you call yourself, it is something that you are. It is, because it is.

"A brother is someone who will give you their last before they have even had their first. He does for you because of who you are not because of what your last name is." I was resting my elbows on the arms of the chair, with my fingers intertwined in front of me and I had my face on my hands. I wasn't looking at the Warden, but I hadn't missed a syllable.

"Look Tarique," I looked up, because that was the first time in five years he'd ever said my first name, "the truth exists, regardless of whether or not we ever become aware of it. You have known in your heart of hearts that you and Shandell were

166

more than friends, you didn't need that man to tell you this. He was your brother because he was." I put my face back down on my hands and I didn't say a word. A few seconds passed and then Warden Vaughan sat back in his chair and said, "Mr. Oakman you may leave now." I got up and left without saying a word.

After the Warden sent me back to my cell I spent all day looking out the window. I knew that Warden Vaughn was right. I had always known that there was a deeper connection between me and Shandell than just friends. If there were ever any doubt, all I needed to do was to think about all the things we shared. Now that he's gone, all of them are significant. I remember spending hours learning the lyrics to songs. The Bee Gees were the hardest to decipher. After *Saturday Night Fever* came out, we stayed up all night trying to decode what in the hell they were saying. We'd mummble high notes until the song got to the chorus, "That night fever, night fever, we know how to do it..." After we gave up, we agreed that they weren't saying anything, they were just whining. We had better luck with rap. In a few days we'd memorized all the words to "Rapper's Delight." Since there were only two of us, we were both "the baby of the bunch." I still don't know what the Bee Gees were saying and for a long time I didn't know why spending all night learning the words to songs was so important, but now I do. What makes them special is that that time and those memories were ours. We truly had loved each other and now, as a result of a combination of decisions can no longer grow together.

As I sit and stare out of my cell's window I begin to focus on what the people outside are doing. I watch them and I realize that I am blaming my father for ruining our lives. My staring is turning into a teary, distant gaze. I've begun to realizes that, as much as I hate to admit it, I have only myself to blame. My father wasn't the person who made me push Shandell through the sliding glass doors. I knew how much Shandell meant to me before the first punch was thrown. I made the decision to act as I did. I made the judgment that what Shandell did to Bria was unforgivable and my decision, followed by my actions, sentenced him to death; no matter what my intensions or feelings for him were.

Staring out my window, time is putting its calming hand on my shoulder and guiding me inward towards the truth. She has patiently watched me as I blamed Bria, my mother, the people around me and finally my father for all that I have gone through. She watched until I ran out of people to blame. This is when she decided to show me that there is only one person left, one who made the decisions, one in the cell and one to blame.

Her guidance has taken me to a different place. Although this place is inside of me, it is strangely unfamiliar to me. I cannot remember ever listening to its rhythm, because I have tuned out the chorus of caring voices led by my mother, Bria, Muggie and Warden Vaughn. Time has shown me that everybody has got to listen at some point, because the truth is impatient and undeniable.

As time takes me deeper, my heart's smooth thubbing slowly unveils the truth to me. Now that I see it, the truth is as familiar as a day and as frightening as a child's first night alone in his new bedroom. The Warden is right, the truth has been there all along I just haven't listened to it. I'd felt it beat in my chest, but my mind was too occupied to pay any attention to it. I was too caught up in satisfying my senses to pay attention to the truth in my feelings. I was too busy chasing the girls and the glory to take the long journey into myself to find the answers I sought in them. Stripped of all of the chaos of my selfishness, I am forced to see and accept the truth, for there is nothing else left.

The truth is becoming clearer during my gaze into the window. The lies that I have told slide like tears on glass. These lies are the justifications that I've given for countless bad decisions. I realize that in the truth there is peace. As the truth's face became clearer and clearer, a calm came over me. The truth I see is me.

All that I was looking for in the girls, on the field and in the blame has always been within me. I have stopped concentrating on the people on the other side of my cell's window now that I have seen the truth. When I look closely at the window, I can see my own reflection. Paying attention to who is doing what outside my window no longer interests me. I want to get to know the truth staring back at me.

I have looked to others for too long for the answers and now

I can finally see that I don't need to look beyond the source of the question for the answer.

The greatest of all endings is the opportunity for a beginning. Through finding my purpose as a teacher and seeing that many of the answers I seek lie within me, I have been given a beginning. As I said earlier, hell is a long way to go to get a lesson. Unfortunately though, too many of us are hard headed. I have lived through my journey to hell. I am one of the fortunate ones. Being held captive by my own decisions has shown me the importance of two things, freedom and each decision.

Too often, when we look at others through windows, we neglect to acknowledge the reflection that is staring back at us. Even through prison bars the truth is plain to see. If we spend less time looking out the window and start paying more attention to the reflection staring back at us, then the truth will never again be beyond our reach. Both the question and the answer start with us. The window pain is the realization that all that is most noticeable in others, good or bad, is so, because it exists within us.

ABOUT THE AUTHOR

The fire that started in the heart of a child born to a teen mother, living in public housing rages on in the man who founded and currently directs an organization that prepares low-income high school students for college.

Steve Perry's commitment to the community began long before he received his masters in social work from the University of Pennsylvania. Even as an undergraduate, he proved that there is more than one road to take to empower the community. Whether working for a US Senator, mayor or presidential candidate as an undergraduate at the University of Rhode Island, or later while serving as director of a homeless shelter, Steve has explored many facets of empowerment.

Perry's commitment and success have not gone unnoticed. He has received several state and regional awards for causes ranging from promoting educational access to low-income students to fighting all forms of sexual violence. Steve Perry has been a candidate for state representative and an adjunct professor, while at the same time serving on numerous regional and local boards.